Helping Kids Hope

A Teacher Explores the Need for Meaning in Our Schools and in Our Lives

Nancy E. Gill

A SCARECROWEDUCATION BOOK

The Scarecrow Press, Inc.
Lanham, Maryland, and Oxford
2003

A SCARECROWEDUCATION BOOK

Published in the United States of America
by Scarecrow Press, Inc.
A Member of the Rowman & Littlefield Publishing Group
4501 Forbes Boulevard, Suite 200, Lanham, MD 20706
www.scarecroweducation.com

PO Box 317
Oxford
OX2 9RU, UK

British Library Cataloguing in Publication Information Available

Library of Congress Cataloging-in-Publication Data

Gill, Nancy E., 1942–
   Helping kids hope : a teacher explores the need for meaning in our schools
and in our lives / Nancy E. Gill.
       p. cm.
   Includes bibliographical references.
   0-8108-4678-0 (pbk. : alk. paper)
   1. Education—Aims and objectives—United States. 2. Motivation in
education—United States.

   LB14.7 .G55 2003
   370.15'4—dc21   2002153541

♾™ The paper used in this publication meets the minimum requirements of
American National Standard for Information Sciences—Permanence of
Paper for Printed Library Materials, ANSI/NISO Z39.48-1992.
Manufactured in the United States of America.

This book is dedicated to my friend, John Linnet, who died June 15, 1997, from cancer, at the age of fifty-four, and who wanted to go on living.

"When dialogue stops, love dies and resentment and hate are born."

—Reuel L. Howe

Contents

Acknowledgments

Thank you to Dorothy Bjarnason, Mary Dayharsh, Catherine Jianopoulos, Jim Brandt, Alfred Hillier, John Spellman, Florence Diesman, Fred Dudley, Remo Fausti, Donald Hiller, and Dyson Shultz, who taught what they were; to S. Leonard Rubinstein, whose vision of what Composition could be made my own vision possible; to Richard Lewis, who showed me what children could do; to all my college students, who were, in so many ways, my teachers—especially to the Literature and Society students who helped to plant the garden, and who gave so much more than three credits could ever measure.

Thank you to each of the younger students I "adopted." Some of you are older now than I was when I first visited you, and have children of your own. It has been a privilege and a blessing to have been part of your life.

Thank you to the administrators, office staff, guidance counselors, and teachers who selected "my kids" and arranged for me to visit them, especially Esther Franklin, Nancy Swisher, Carol Giger, and Joan Varonka; to the English Department and the Human Relations Committee, whose funding made those visits possible; to the Office of Social Equity of the State System of Higher Education, which funded my summer project. Special thanks to Ruth Schwimmer, Sam Bidleman, Dee Anne Casteel, Don Gross, Joe Klusman, and Thomas Lynch, who let me wander so freely through their classrooms and their schools.

Thank you to The International Society For Exploring Teaching Alternatives (ISETA), especially to Bill Mullin, Gloria Balderrama, Linc Fisch, Charlie Wales, Jim Marlin, Christine Campbell, Ken Klopfenstein,

Jane Wolfle, and Susan Moncada, for providing more than ten years of support and encouragement.

Thank you to all the faculty, students, parents, and townspeople who supported, contributed to, or participated in my special projects, especially to the parents, for allowing their children to participate, and to Karl and Ginny Beamer, George Agbango, Linda LeMura, Cathy Livengood, Chris Alichnie, Robert Campbell, Fredda Massari-Novak, Keri Torphy, Lara Peterson, Kathleen Hartman, Judy Reick, Robin Arrington, Donna David, DuAne Davis, Linda George, and Michelle Lewis. Very special thanks to Ardie Kissinger and his family, to Melissa Brown and her family, to Terry and Lou Ann Sharrow and their family, and to Sean Miller and Lormont Sharp and their families, for their courage, and their good will.

Thank you to Marlin Wagner, for photographing the third grade class, to Dena Lake for writing about us in *The Germantown Leader*, to *The Press-Enterprise* for publishing my letter about the writing workshop, to Bob Bomboy for contacting regional televisin stations, and to Shareen Silva for her articles and photographs in *The Voice.*

Thank you to John Linnet, Anna Romanofsky, Phil and Lorraine Engstrom, Gordon Ross, Gertrud Hogberg, Susan Kroll-Smith, Riley Smith, Anne Foulke, Jean Hawk, Melanie Dworsak, Betsy Haney, Bonita Rhone, Jack Fiorini, Jack Roberts, David Rein, Hsien-Tung Liu, Doug Goerlitz, Donna Yaniga, Nancy Nash, Jim Fetterman, Pia Snyder, Kerstin Barrett, Linnae Wintersteen, Pat Parker, Leighow Veterinary Hospital, Bill and Marion Koch, Connor Printing, L & M Stationery, Reichart Lumber, Bob and Marge Eshleman, Cathy Torsell, Lenka and Sabah Salih, Ekema Agbaw, Gerry Dullea and Ervene Gulley, Irvin Wright, Tony Sylvester, Mary Harris, Ken and Inez Lundemo, Cindy Cuzick, and Dee DeHaem for so many years of listening.

Thank you to Barbara Burton, Lynn and Phil Keiner, Sandy Newman, Dena Lake, John Pizzola, Paul Dubeck, Lushington Fletcher, Mary Lou Fisher, Chris St. Clair, and Bill Hecker, for your support, encouragement, appreciation, and friendship, and for your hope, which has lasted a long time, in spite of everything that has made hope so difficult.

Thank you to my editors, Cindy Tursman and John Calderone, for your patience and helpfulness.

Permissions

I am grateful for permission to use quotations from the following sources:

S. Leonard Rubinstein, "Composition: A Collision with Literature," *College English* 27 (January 1966), pp. 273–277. Used with permission of the National Council of Teachers of English.

Complete Poems of Robert Frost, 1949 (New York: Henry Holt and Company, 1949). Reprinted by permission of Henry Holt and Company, LLC.

Robert Frost: The Years of Triumph, 1915–1938 by Lawrance Thompson. Copyright © 1970 by Lawrance Thompson. Reprinted by permission of Henry Holt and Company, LLC.

Excerpts from pp. 104, 120, 121 from *The Art of Loving* by Erich Fromm. Copyright © 1956 by Erich Fromm. Copyright renewed © 1984 by Annis Fromm. Reprinted by permission of HarperCollins Publishers Inc.

From *One Flew Over the Cuckoo's Nest* by Ken Kesey. Copyright © 1962, 1990 by Ken Kesey. Used by permission of Viking Penguin, a division of Penguin Putnam Inc.

From *One Flew Over the Cuckoo's Nest*. Reprinted by permission of Sterling Lord Literistic, Inc. Copyright © 1962, 1990, 2002 by Ken Kesey and the Estate of Ken Kesey.

From "A Clean, Well-Lighted Place." Reprinted with permission of Scribner, an imprint of Simon & Schuster Adult Publishing Group, from *The Short Stories of Ernest Hemingway.* Copyright © 1933 by Charles Scribner's Sons. Copyright renewed © 1961 by Mary Hemingway.

From *The First 49 Stories* by Ernest Hemingway, published by Jonathan Cape. Reprinted by permission of the Random House Group Ltd.

From Richard Lewis, ed., *Miracles: Poems By Children of the English-Speaking World* (New York: Simon & Schuster, Inc., 1966). "My Poem" (16), "The

Introduction

When I first began teaching at my university, many literature students came to class drunk, or high, and some freshman composition students did as well. They came without their books, without having read their books. They came without their papers, without having written their papers. Sometimes they sat on benches out in the hall, writing what they were planning to turn in when class started. Male students leaned back in their seats, stretched their legs out into the aisles, crossed their arms on their chests, rolled their eyes, told me in every way they could that they knew this was not where they belonged, or where they wanted to be.

I had never encountered students who weren't sober in class, or students who lay sprawled on the floor in the halls between classes, caressing their girlfriends and boyfriends when I arrived in the morning. Students at my previous university had not skipped class by the dozen on Fridays, had not left the campus every weekend to party, had not bragged about vomiting and urinating on lawns, having sex with strangers, scattering beer cans from one end of town to the other.

I had never met students who had put off freshman composition until their junior or senior years, who considered it a matter of pride that they had never been inside the library, had never read a book "all the way through." I had never imagined having a college class that could not read a first grade children's story, had never had entire classes of students whose SAT Verbal scores were in the 300 range, or lower.

At first, I naively assumed that what these students needed from me was encouragement—that is, the same kind of encouragement that I had responded to, as a student, and a teacher, not so many years before: encouragement to be what I most deeply was, and not what anyone else believed I should be; encouragement to speak from the most introspective and most quiet place inside, without trying to impress or flatter, and without feeling any need to placate or manipulate; encouragement to listen for that same authentic, courageous, unmistakable voice in others.

But such encouragement, so important and heartfelt to me, meant nothing to my new students, who skipped class as often as they attended, who rarely participated in discussions, who cheated on term papers, turning in perfectly typed packets of generic material on how to do or understand just about anything.

No, students at my previous university were not like this, never imagined being like this, considered themselves "real students," came prepared almost every day, participated in class eagerly, with no prompting at all, discussed, not just with me, but with each other, stayed long after class to discuss, followed me, and other professors, to the student union, where we spent the noon hour discussing, helped organize marathon discussions for the entire campus, discussions that went on for hours, and involved not just English students and faculty, but secretaries, librarians, coaches, biologists, psychology professors, spouses, and townspeople.

The course that generated so much engagement at my first university was entitled "The Need For Meaning." It was a freshman composition course, required of all students at that university. It was nothing like any course any of us had ever taught, or taken, before.

Designed by S. Leonard Rubinstein, "The Need For Meaning" course syllabus contained nothing about sentence structure, paragraphs, unity, coherence, spelling, grammar, punctuation, vivid verbs, vivid adjectives, or any of that. It consisted of a list of half a dozen texts, beginning with "A Clean, Well-Lighted Place," by Ernest Hemingway, and *Ecclesiastes*, and ending with Dostoevsky's *The Grand Inquisitor*. With this list came perhaps fifty pages of assumptions, questions, and guidelines for discussion and papers.

The composition teacher, Mr. Rubinstein explained, uses literature to teach writing, but he uses it in a "peculiar and primitive way. . . . [He] has to return to the savage need which produces art and which makes art meaningful. . . . He and his student begin—not with the condition of literature—but with the condition of mortality. . . . Death, birth, sickness, need, hunger, pain, death. We exist and we end. Why?" (Rubinstein 1966, 273).

My colleagues and I studied this syllabus together, took it to dinner, sat with it in local restaurants, sat in our offices, reading it aloud to each other, decided that we would open our classes to each other, that we would all behave as students, would all, that is, *be* students, explore the readings, and explore Rubinstein's questions as if our *lives*, not our *jobs*, depended on them, which, indeed, they did.

We decided that we would wander freely in and out of each other's classes, participate in each other's discussions, show the students, as clearly and completely as we could, that we were not "above" them, that we did not believe we had answers *for* them, that we did not want them to have, or seem to have, *our* answers at all. We were asking them to explore as we explored, to explore *with* us, not *for* us. Certain that we did not regard writing or discussion as a performance, as a clever little dance for a grade, we were determined to create a classroom climate characterized by absolute respect for the mind and spirit of every person, for the dignity of every person. We would do our best to become facilitators of learning, and of clear, articulate, and meaningful writing, for ourselves and for our students. We hoped our classes could become places where introspection and dialogue felt comfortable and natural—and of central importance for all of us.

What I wanted to do at my second institution, more than anything else, was to create "Need For Meaning" classes there, but I could find no one who saw teaching and learning in the way Rubinstein had enabled me to see them. Colleagues were not at all interested, and students, for the most part, were not prepared to take their minds, or their teachers' minds, so seriously.

My schooling, and my life, had not prepared me for students like these. At first, my dismay, my disappointment, and my anxiety over not being able to make any meaningful connection with so many of them were so painful that I felt overwhelmed by my own misery. I didn't want to give up teaching, but I could hardly call what I did "teaching," I thought, if my students were as miserable as I was, and if they could not bring themselves to tell me, or show me, what they needed from me.

I was quite sure about what they *didn't* need from me: They didn't need Literature of the Western World, and they didn't need composition readers that they couldn't read and couldn't appreciate. They didn't need more experiences of failure, and they didn't need to be reminded, daily, of all their past emotional, intellectual, and academic failings.

I was also quite sure that much of their overindulgence in drugs and alcohol said something about their inability to deal with their own pain, but I had no experience with alcohol and drugs, or with academic failure. I had never been one to deny how I felt. I had spent my youth examining my life, trying to learn from it. I had been open to virtually all of my teachers, had approached reading, writing, and discussion eagerly, had loved books of all kinds, and had read books of my own choosing since I was a small child.

Most of my students had done none of this. Perhaps, I thought, they didn't know how to begin, they didn't know what their strengths might be, what potential they might have, and they didn't know what *might* have meaning for them. The pain they felt made it almost impossible for them to feel hopeful enough to look beyond it.

I, then, I decided, must find a way to look beyond *mine*, to see and understand how theirs came to be. If they couldn't tell me, well, maybe I could find out some other way.

I began visiting area schools, observing, first and then, gradually, talking with students, asking them questions I wished my college students could answer. I received permission to visit a gifted third grade class for a year, twice a week, and to take over the class when I wished. I saw, from my first day in third grade, what I had never realized. I saw that independence, imagination, creativity, honesty, energy, humor, playfulness, confidence, and so many other things I took for granted were not valued there, were, in fact, routinely criticized and punished.

Because of this discovery, I stayed with the gifted students for the next ten years, to do what I could to protect and nurture their spirits as long as they were in school. I visited their classes when that was possible, and regularly took them out of study hall to listen to them individually and in small groups. I attended their football and basketball games, and their plays and concerts. I chaperoned class trips, invited them to my house, and, sometimes, visited their homes. I did everything I could to show them that I would be there when they needed someone to listen, and when they didn't.

When they graduated, their high school principal invited me to work with the school's new ninth graders who, he said, were hostile and uncooperative, and nothing like this first group. Finding these students to be almost identical to those I had come to know so well, I called half a dozen high schools across the state and asked to work with students whom teachers regarded as "problems"—students who abused drugs and alcohol, who came from dysfunctional homes, who appeared most often in in-school suspension, who were failing. I asked for a total of "about a hundred," because, at first, I had no released time, and no funding, but all schools, large and small, rural and urban, said they had many more students who fit my description. I stayed with these students for four years, treating them exactly as I had treated the students labeled gifted. Almost all of them graduated, and a number of those who did not earned their GED.

I went on to "adopt" two groups of approximately sixty students each at a large "inner city" high school, staying with each group for four years, this time taking my college students with me and arranging for the younger, almost exclusively African American, students to become pen pals with my students and with other, mostly white, high school students, and to participate in projects at the college and elsewhere with them.

All of these students became my teachers. They made it possible for me to see how school felt, how living felt, to see what mattered to them, and to respond to what mattered in ways that also mattered to me.

The students I met in third grade are thirty-five years old now. They have no notes and tapes from that time, don't remember what I remember, and look forward to becoming reacquainted with the parts of themselves they left behind. Many of them now have children of their own, who will have their own third grades to remember, and forget. I hope that, when they are old enough, and ready, there will be a "Need For Meaning" class waiting for them. In the meantime, may consciousness and courage be their companions, and may their griefs be small.

CHAPTER 1

"In Much Wisdom Is Much Grief":
Thinking about Teaching as Learning

"IN MUCH WISDOM IS MUCH GRIEF"

"In much wisdom is much grief," says the author of *Ecclesiastes*, "and he who increases knowledge increases sorrow." In my youth, I knew I didn't have "much wisdom," but I did have "much grief," and I didn't know what to do with it, how to talk about it, or even whether to talk about it. I had never heard anyone else, child or adult, talk about grief. My mother had spent months in the hospital and had nearly died of peritonitis when I was five, and my sister and I had been separated and sent to live with relatives. None of them had ever cried in our presence, or expressed any sadness, or offered any comfort to us. We were simply extra persons in their households, extra burdens. They made it clear that we were to be quiet, to do what they said, and to stay out of their way. They did not speak, except to give orders or reprimands. They seemed not to know how to talk with children at all, seemed not to give any thought to their own emotional lives, or to ours.

As a child, and as a teenager, I had attended a Protestant church. I had never heard a sermon on grief there, or discussed grief in a Sunday School class. None of my teachers in public school had ever mentioned it either.

As a small child, I had stood patiently next to my mother, looking up at her, so many times. "I hurt myself," I would announce, holding my hand up for her inspection. "Nonsense," she would say. "There's nothing there." What I wanted was for her to stop making biscuits, or rolling out pie crust, wipe her floured hands on her apron, and give me a hug, but she never did. She never hugged us for any reason, never asked how we felt, never offered an observation that suggested that she had given thought to how we felt. My sister and I, even in first and second grade, hugged *her* when she cried, wrapped our small arms around her knees, and told her everything would be okay, but everything was not okay, and we didn't know what to do about it. "Gills don't cry," my father said once, when I was in high school. "This one does," I answered matter-of-factly. Later, when I began attending the local college, he drove me to class. On an impulse one day, as I was getting out of the car, I announced, almost in a whisper, "You know, Dad, I smile and laugh a lot, but I'm really a very unhappy person." He was startled, dismayed, angry, defensive. "Don't ever say anything like that again," he said. "It suggests that I wasn't a perfect parent."

In February of that same year, our debate coach, whom we loved and respected more than anyone we had ever met, learned that he had terminal cancer. "Mr. Hillier asked me to tell you," his wife said. "He hopes to complete the year, and to attend every debate tournament, especially the National Tournament in Stockton, California."

Tearfully, we asked what we might do for him, how we might help him.

"Just go on as you have been," she said, "and he will do the same. He knows that he is important to you, but what you may not know is that you are just as important to him. You are what gives his life meaning."

We had not thought of it that way before. We thought of it that way now, and every day we watched him as he walked down the hall, slowly, carefully, as if he were thinking about something else. He continued to debate each of us, one at a time, without notes. He continued to critique our arguments, calmly, graciously, focusing always on our strengths—never rude, never impatient, never sarcastic, never the slightest bit defensive. He continued to attend tournaments.

Now, we saw, his clothes hung on him; his skin became jaundiced. Now he carried a glass of water everywhere. The hand with the glass in it shook. In Stockton, he was too weak to leave the motel, but he was there, and every evening we gathered in the motel dining room for supper, sitting at the same table each time. Carved in the beam over our table was this line: "I shall pass this way but once. Any goodness I can do, any kindness I can show, let me do it now, for I shall not pass this way again."

On the last day of class, we attended the college award ceremony. Mr. Hillier sat in a straight-backed chair on the stage near a small table that held his glass of water. He called each of us up to praise us for our work with him, for the events we had entered and the trophies we had won. No one praised him for *his* accomplishments. No one announced that he had made it through the year for us, that he had taken the only time he had to debate and advise each of us, that he had attended every tournament, that his love for us had made all our achievements possible. He died the next day, having done everything he had set out to do. At the memorial service, we learned that he had even written his own eulogy. "Do not weep for me," it began. "I have had the life I wanted. There is nothing I would have changed—except its length."

As a beginning teacher, I thought about grief, and was so grateful, at last, to find a place to put some of it. Students at my first university, in our "Need For Meaning" class, listened the way I had always hoped someone would listen. My colleagues listened. They had griefs of their own to share. In spite of the fact that none of us had discussed our griefs in the ways in which we were discussing them now, we seemed to know how to speak, and how to listen, in ways that created enough space and warmth. We did not attack, or criticize, did not even advise, but, instead, listened and asked questions—to see, to know, to empathize, to understand.

As we thought together about the readings, and about our emotional and intellectual lives, we built trust. As we built trust, we shared more. We looked at both the authors and the characters of our texts as persons like ourselves, persons with layer upon layer of thought, feeling, observation, experience—all there to scrutinize, to draw upon, to connect, to learn from.

It was heady stuff. Students reported that they couldn't sleep at night, that they lay awake, thinking about our class, our readings, and our lives. What we were experiencing was so far—so far—from what they had expected in a college class.

"I don't know how you get your optimism," one older student wrote to me. "I wish I had it. To me, the world is such an ugly, repulsive place. I could never bring children into it. In spite of your life, you don't see it that way. What is it that makes that possible?"

A young woman wrote that she had never felt confident about her writing, had always admired others for their abilities, had always assumed that her life was too boring to write about. Our reading and discussion reminded her of her father, of how much she loved and admired him, reminded her of the farm on which she had grown up, told her that this place of her youth was far from boring, was, in fact, her world, and was worth the time and attention she was now free to give it. She brought her finished paper to me, a piece of magic, she said it was, a paper that seemed to write itself for her, a paper that had her living, breathing father in it. Every time she read it, he was there. How could that be? Perhaps, if she kept writing, other people could be there as well. Her life now, she said, looked different, felt different. It was the same life as before. How could she ever have thought it was boring?

ALICE IN WHERE?

For three years, I dreamed about remodeling churches—huge, beautiful, dark, wood churches. I climbed into organ lofts, looked down on beautiful, quiet, holy sanctuaries, with pencil, hammer, saw, nails, and two-by-fours in hand. And I was not alone. There were dozens of other carpenters, all working, as I was, to bring these churches up to date, all pausing, at times, to stand in awe of the light slanting through stained glass windows, all doing their best not to block the light.

And then, in my dreams, I was, suddenly, hiking alone in the dark. It was raining. I was tired. I had been hiking for days, months, years. I didn't know how long. It is, after all, hard to measure time in the dark, and besides, under such conditions, time seems to lose whatever meaning it used to have, or seemed to have.

I saw a red-brick mall off to my right, across a parking lot, and I turned, hurried in that direction, aimed to take shelter under the roof overhang. I reached the wall, leaned against it, sighed with relief, closed my eyes for a second, realized, suddenly, that a cement truck had appeared, out of nowhere. There were no other vehicles in the parking lot. I was not standing near a doorway. And yet, here was this cement truck—backing up, backing up, backing up—coming in my direction, coming straight for me. I called out, "Hey! I'm *here*! Hey! Look out!" It didn't look out. I slid out of the way, just in time.

I dreamed that I was walking down the main street of a familiar town, an old town, with dilapidated, empty storefronts. I came to an old wooden, graffiti-covered factory, with rows of broken windows, and walked alongside it. It was as quiet as Sunday, no one but me on the street. I reached the corner at last, turned, and was dismayed to find that the factory turned the corner as well, extended down another seemingly endless street. I walked for days, for months. The street and the factory stretched on and on.

It began to rain. I had no umbrella, no windbreaker, only a thin raincoat. I was shivering. At last I reached the end of it. And there, the road abruptly ended, faded into thick brown mud, wet grass, weeds. There were several pieces of bright yellow road-building equipment parked there. On one of them, Benjamin Franklin and Benjamin Banneker sat together, engaged in conversation. Both of them smiled at me, called me by name. "Hello," they said. "You see that the road over the next mountain has not been built yet. Join us, why don't you? No point heading over that mountain alone at this time of year. Wait, with us, for the weather to clear!" I climbed up beside them.

In some dreams, thousands of identical dried, unfired clay objects came in on endless conveyor belts, passed me, and went out in the same condition they arrived in. In others, I walked along endless rivers, walked for miles at a time, never saw anyone on my side. All the people were on the other side. They were all talking at once, like a crowd waiting for department stores to open in the mall so they could rush in and find a bargain.

I was looking for bridges. There weren't any. I decided I had to make my own bridges. I made dozens, hundreds, worked day and night. I made wide, strong stone and concrete bridges, room for dozens, hundreds, of people at a time. I sank the piers into the river bottom myself, lowered steel forms onto them, poured my own concrete. I made beautiful wooden bridges, works of art, where two or three at a time could gather, go fishing, admire the view. I built halfway out into the river, three-fourths of the way, nine-tenths of the way across, called out to the people on the other side, "Say! Here's a good bridge! Come! Build your share! We can talk! We can exchange views! We can travel together!" They went on talking to each other, did not look at me, showed no sign that they knew, or cared, that these bridges—and I—were there.

It was twenty years before I succeeded in building even one bridge. In all that time, I met no other travelers. At last, someone spoke to me, though only briefly. After that, I moved away from rivers, climbed huge stone mountains, bent close to the earth, realized that the stones under my feet had writing on them, realized that the writing was in Hebrew. I deciphered it slowly, a few words a year. "Why rush?" I asked myself. I couldn't think of an answer. Again, I saw no other travelers, though, for brief moments, I thought I heard laughter and light chatter far below me. I reached a high plateau, a meadow filled with flowers—beautiful, beyond description. I walked among the flowers, admired all of them, took my time, rested. From where I was, I could see nothing but mountains, each with sharp, jagged peaks and no snow. I looked in every direction. There was no path ahead of me, and as I looked back over the miles I had already traveled, I could not see any route where I might retrace my steps.

I dreamed that two vultures visited my class. They sat together next to the door, each of their wings more than six feet long. They draped them awkwardly behind a row of students, behind me, watched me with their vulture eyes. The students glanced at them, hunkered down in their seats, didn't know what to do, thought they were there to eat them, looked at me, hoped I would protect them, if it came to that, breathed thirty sighs of relief when the vultures left.

I dreamed of a huge church, surrounded by empty picnic tables, the streets around the church filled with hungry African Americans of all ages. I saw the church women, who were white, laying out silverware and empty plates on all the tables, heard the white minister giving the blessing. No one, black or white, sat at the tables, and no food was served. The church women waited a while, and then picked up all the silverware and plates, washed them, and put them away.

I dreamed of huge empty warehouses surrounded by manicured green grass, connected by concrete sidewalks. Students passed from one to another, endlessly.

I dreamed of the entrance to the subway in Philadelphia, another massive concrete structure—dirty, unlighted, filled with trash. All my students were lined up there, their hands outstretched, their palms open. I had only one dollar left. Where, how, could I give it? For whom would it do any good?

SOWS' EARS

An administrator at my new institution called me into his office, told me that my students were sows' ears. It was my first year there. I didn't know if they were sows' ears or not, but I defended them, said they had promise, said when they trusted me they wrote thoughtfully, honestly, clearly. No matter, he said. This was a C college, and I gave too many B's and A's. B's and A's were grade inflation. Grade inflation was not good at a C college. He was warning me. I must give C's. I must also give D's, and E's, and F's, and G's, and all the rest. I said I surely would, if they wrote so poorly as all that, but I would continue to aim for B's, because B's were a lot more fun than C's and D's and the others. B's meant students knew how to make themselves memorable. I wanted to encourage memorableness, didn't want my students to be average, to blend in with the masses, didn't want my classes to be unmemorable either. Life was too short to spend it like that.

Most of my students understood this, told me they had had enough boring lectures about semicolons and topic sentences, about emphasis and coherence, about conjunctions and vivid verbs. They said they had never heard an interesting lecture on such matters and couldn't imagine one. I couldn't either, though I sometimes gave them an imitation lecture, just to learn how well they did or didn't take notes. They were rather pleased to learn that I didn't want them to put on any airs they weren't used to, and, that first year, treated me to glimpses of dorm life as it really was. They talked about nothing much with more energy than it deserved, but showed me, that way, what they had not yet thought of putting in their backpacks.

You don't rush in, they said, and start spilling your guts to strangers. That's not how we do things here. You start light, throw your beer bottle out into the ring, see if it gets shot at. You follow with yourself—maybe, someday.

It made sense to me. However, I said, we have only fifteen weeks. How could I put up with all those beer bottles? We need a way to move a little faster, get beyond what costs us nothing to throw out. Life is short.

Yeah, yeah, they said. They were not convinced. When seventy-five out of eighty composition students cheated on their term papers that semester, turned in dead and flawless volumes about how to play golf, how to read Poe, and how to read Kierkegaard, subjects our class had never discussed and would never be likely to discuss, I figured it was at least forty-nine percent my fault, because I had told them they were free to explore any subject that had meaning for them, but I hadn't told them what "explore" meant, and what "meaning" meant. I had assumed they knew, had assumed it was just a matter of trust, as they had said.

I read all eighty papers, as if some human being within driving distance of the college had written them, as if that human being might really read my comments and might really care. I put a grade on the five papers my students had written, but put no grade at all on the others. I explained why, and announced that I would be in my office the rest of the day if anyone wished to complain about the grade, or lack of grade. Not one complained. Not one.

Two weeks later, I received a late paper, copied exactly from one of those plagiarized papers I had just returned. I explained that I had already read that same document, and that it had not been original the first time. This student looked at me, I must confess, with swinish eyes, and said nothing. On his final, he wrote his philosophy of cheating. He was a wrestler, he said, and wrestlers were good at wrestling, not writing. Some of his non-wrestling buddies knew how to write. It was an even trade. He taught them to wrestle; they wrote for him. After all, he said, he wanted to become a teacher, and coach wrestling. Only this English class stood in his way.

Not all my students were wrestlers. Not all wrestlers shared his philosophy. But it was clear to me that the word would get around, and that, if I didn't change my ways, I'd have to read about such subjects as golf, Poe, and Kierkegaard all over again the next semester.

I laid out an anti-cheating plan, which I used for the next quarter of a century, and expressed my sympathy for all those who dreaded writing a term paper of any kind. "Divide and conquer," I told all my students every semester after that first one. "If fifteen pages makes you anxious, think three parts. Think one part at a time. If formality scares you, think *informality*. Think *Before*, *During*, and *After*. In the *Before* section, tell me what you already know about your subject, why you want to know more, and what, exactly, you are hoping to know. Write this as if you are sitting across the table from me in the Student Union. Try to imagine that I might doubt your sincerity, given my experience last semester. Make it clear that nobody else could possibly have known or cared about these things. In *During*, explore what others know—that is, go out, like Lewis and Clark, head up your wide Missouri, carry your own canoes between rivers, reach your own Pacific, show me your route, describe the scenery along the way. In *After*, reflect on your trip, ask yourself if it was worth it, and consider where you would go next, if you had it in you to travel further."

I was aware of only two casualties along this route. One said he had surveyed hundreds of books on gun control and could not find one single book or magazine *for* it in our library, or anywhere else. All of them were against it, as he was.

The other invented half a dozen issues of *Sports Illustrated* that did not exist to save himself the trouble of having to enter the library, which was right next door to our building, within easy portage for me, if not for him. I told him I scoured the library for those issues with no success. His reply was that his buddy had taken them home with him.

In class, he protested. Why should he write the truth for me? He had no respect for me. And why was that? Well, because, frankly, I was not a millionaire, and he put no stock in people, male or female, who were not millionaires. "You got me there," I said. "I am not a millionaire—nor do I plan or expect to be one. But tell me the name of a millionaire within driving distance of this university, and I'll invite him or her to class. Then we can all learn from this person."

Well, it just so happened, he said, that he mowed the lawn of a local millionaire every week, and he immediately gave me his telephone number. When I called, though, the millionaire's wife said he was taking a shower, and, anyway, she was sure he had no interest in being part of a freshman composition class. We had to settle for someone else who loved money, recommended by another student. Just to liven things up a bit, I also invited someone the same age who lived more modestly, and who, I knew, would be an outspoken advocate of building connections between parents and parents, and parents and their children, no matter how much money they had, or didn't have.

Well, two casualties in a quarter of a century—that's not so bad. And I never read another paper about golf, or Poe, or Kierkegaard in all that time. Unfortunately, though, my students wrote a lot of B papers, and, of course, I knew that that was very bad for a place with a reputation as a C college, and I knew I would have to pay some kind of price for thinking so highly of most of my students. But what could they do to me, really? After all, everyone believed in academic freedom these days. You couldn't go around telling other teachers what grades to give, or how to evaluate papers, and that sort of thing—could you? I mean, this was higher education, and there's nothing high about that.

E-DUCERE

It is a sad thing when you want to teach and learn, when you want to read and discuss and explore, and you find that your students want to sleep late and throw frisbees and party every evening, and go home on the weekends, especially when your classes meet at four o'clock on Friday afternoons and at eight o'clock every morning, which, you discover, is the class schedule reserved for new faculty such as yourself. If all the students were there at the same time, there would be approximately forty of them in a room built for twenty-five. At the beginning, you think that this will be your most difficult and challenging problem, but it is nothing compared with your other problems. It is like worrying about a dead fly on the windowsill during a plague of frogs or locusts. You think it is the end of the world, and your first impulse is to take cover in the basement, but you cannot do that, because these frogs and locusts are your responsibility.

I told my eighty students in Literature of the Western World that Erich Fromm, the author of a wonderful little book called *The Art of Loving,* explained very well the root meaning of the word "education." The infinitive form, he said, was *e-ducere,* which, in his view, meant "to lead forth, or to bring out something which is potentially present" (Fromm 1956, 104). What this meant was that the student was not merely an empty bag into which the professor poured information. It meant that the student was, instead, a sort of seed that the professor tried to help sprout.

This went over about as well as a recitation of *Beowulf* in the original Old English. These students didn't want anything to be led forth from or even to them. What was I thinking?! Literature of the Western World was required of business majors.

"Now, I ask you," they said, "do business majors have any need for a course such as this? Certainly not. Business majors have a need for business courses. Period."

So—they were here because the course was required. It was not required that they engage themselves with the course material. It was only required that they pass and have the grade recorded on their transcripts. It wasn't *their* fault that the course was required. They leaned back, closed their eyes, covered their faces with the campus paper, and hoped I might find a way to make *The Iliad*, Greek tragedy, and snippets of the Bible entertaining enough to rouse them from their collective slumbers.

It's a pity I couldn't laugh in those days. My students frightened and saddened me. What could I possibly do with them? Later, I realized that I could simply *tell* them that they saddened and frightened me, but at the beginning, that option wasn't obvious. I tried what I thought might be "common sense" instead.

"Well," I said. "These selections are, in the editors' estimation, the most important writings in Europe prior to the time of Shakespeare. I don't know of anything that's being written now that's going to last hundreds of years—that's going to be required reading in the year 2000, or 3000—or even in 1969."

No comment.

I went on. "It might be interesting to take a look at them and see if we can tell why they've lasted this long, or why they're required of you. After all, it was not the English department that made this requirement. It was the business department."

No comment.

I described the Classics of the Western World course that I had taken as a senior English major, and explained how my professor had asked us to approach these works. "Imagine," he had said, "that, even though you have never considered these subjects before, you instinctively know how to think about them. Do not summarize the plots. Do not even describe the characters. Instead, stand farther back, and consider what your own definition of *art* and *artistry* might be. Then use these works to support your definition."

Art and artistry were not subjects that could hold my students' attention.

My students did not know how to care about literature that was "so old." It was not enough for them that their professor might find these writings interesting. Nothing I said helped them to find a way into the readings. They would not read them, and campus requirements prevented them from dropping the course. "What are we supposed to do?" one boy asked, thoroughly frustrated. "Become the manager of some classy company, take a client out to dinner, and ask if he's read *The Iliad*?"

A few semesters later, I would have learned how to let go of my anxiety. I would have found some ways to listen better to theirs, would have asked them to imagine talking to clients—and talking to spouses, and children as well—but at first, that possibility didn't occur to me either. I concluded only that the course should not be required of business majors, that, for students outside of English at least, it should be an elective. A dozen students disappeared after the first few days of class, and did not return until the date of the first exam, specified in the department syllabus. They returned expecting what they had heard other professors used—a multiple-choice, true and false exam, but discovered that classmates who attended regularly all had their own journals to which they referred, and on which they based their open-book essays. Those who had skipped class had still not read *any* of the assignments. They couldn't tell *The Iliad* from *Agamemnon*, didn't know the Old Testament from the New. They sat in class, copying the introductory material in the text, as their exam.

After that, some came to class drunk, or high. Many arrived drunk at the final exam, with nothing to say and no way to pass the course. I felt I had failed them. I had not been able to speak their language, or even to translate it, and they had not been able to appreciate mine. We made no connection at all, and the literature, which had seemed so rich and important to me as a student, seemed, now, a huge burden that I was required to "teach" and that my students were required to "take." I added this experience to my pile of grief, and asked that, if possible, I not be assigned that course again.

HIGHER EDUCATION

I didn't know then that if the right wheels of your car drop off the roadway onto the berm, you should not immediately try to turn back onto the road, but should proceed straight ahead at a reduced speed. I learned this lesson on a Sunday, the last weekend of the spring semester before Final Exam Week of the first year at my new school. When I woke, and found myself in a body cast in the hospital, I did not consider this a catastrophe. I thought of it as a challenge and an adventure. The catastrophe had been the previous academic year—when I discovered, unfortunately, rather belatedly, that all colleges were not the same, and that all teachers could not reach all students.

I didn't understand why so many of my students, and so many of my colleagues as well, used alcohol to help them through the pain they felt about failing to teach and learn. I didn't understand why they spent so much time bragging about how much they drank, or about how badly they had behaved at the last party. I didn't want anything to numb the pain I felt. I just wanted to understand it and find better ways to respond to students like those I had not been able to reach the semester before.

The other patients on my floor in the hospital looked at me with a kind of awe. They preferred their abdominal surgery, their heart attacks, their strokes, their diabetes to a few broken bones and a body full of bruises—which heal—and which hurt, granted, but which don't hurt anywhere near as much as emotional heartache, which sometimes never heals, no matter what anyone says or does.

The physical injury happened quickly—in a few seconds, a minute or two, at the most. All of me crossed my long Volvo-122 gearshift and fell into the floor on the passenger side of the car—my only voyage, ever, without a seatbelt. The newspaper article, which I read weeks later, said I was driving too fast for conditions. That wasn't true. It was that I didn't know how to drive on the berm, didn't realize I might *have* to know. I broke my femur, my shoulder, and my nose, and had whiplash so bad that my spine lost its curves at both ends. The car swirled around and slammed into a pole. Window glass shattered into tiny bits and rained over me. In and out of consciousness, I told myself to keep my mouth shut and my eyes closed, so it wouldn't rain in. The driver ahead of me watched these things in his rearview mirror and called the police and the ambulance. That was it.

I woke up a few days later and found myself in traction, being prepared for surgery. It was a pleasure. Ask anyone who's been there and survived. It is a pleasure to open your eyes and realize that they work, to flex your muscles and realize that they hurt, that they are alive. It is a wonderful gift to find that you can think and talk and eat and, eventually, remember almost everything that happened, that you can imagine, and work toward, a time when you will be reasonably whole and functional again. The nearness of the possibility that things might have turned out very differently rearranges all your previous priorities, colors them new colors, gives you a chance to do some interior decorating that you might, otherwise, not have known how to do.

I spent three months in the hospital, in the body cast, and had a beautiful, memorable, miraculous, happy time. No more literature students who didn't want to come to class, who didn't want to read their books, who didn't want to learn anything that I was required, in that class, to teach. No more composition students plagiarizing on their term papers. No more colleagues telling me I shouldn't use this text, shouldn't use this theme topic, shouldn't use journals, shouldn't take students on field trips, shouldn't speak up, shouldn't have a view others didn't share. No more.

Instead, I had a wonderful, hearing-impaired, seventy-some-year-old roommate who also had been in a car accident, who laughed at my jokes, who thought my jokes helped her get well. Instead, I had student nurses from my former university who arranged a party in my honor so all the patients on the wing could meet me. Instead, I had a room full of patients, after that, all of them talking enthusiastically, not about illness and injury and death and loss, but about life, about the things that gave life meaning. Instead, I had a night nurse who woke me up almost every night, just to talk, because she had heard about the conversations we had during the day, and wanted to be included in them. Instead, I had a lonely, grandfatherly visitor from a room down the hall, who at first had not responded to treatment for his heart attack, and who now got up, dressed himself, and went to the cafeteria for two pieces of lemon meringue pie, one for each of us, at seven o'clock in the morning. Instead, I had dozens of visits from students, colleagues, and townspeople, from my first teaching position, all of them full of ideas and full of life, and happy to see me. What was so surprising about it was that all these people came, not so much to cheer me up, but to be part of something that cheered *them* up. They came asking *me* for advice, for encouragement, for hope — and it was all because, on the outside, I looked so injured, and on the inside, I was so grateful and happy, and they thought I should feel sorry for myself, but I didn't. It was all because they passed around stories about me, and then came to talk, and generated more stories.

The student nurse who gave me vitamin shots every day or so in my left arm, the only part of me that wasn't injured or protected by the cast, told how she practiced on me, how I was her first real patient, after the orange. And I told about her — that first time — how she aimed at my arm, how she brought her arm down, again and again, before she could finally bring herself to ease that long needle into my skin, and about the doctor, who rebroke my nose with a mallet, one night after supper, in order to straighten it. One of the friends I had been staying with told me of her own hospital experience, many years ago, when she came to have her only daughter by natural childbirth, how proud she was, how excited, how focused—until she realized by the look on the nurse's face that something was not right, that something was terribly wrong—and learned that her only daughter, for whom she had struggled so hard and so well, had been stillborn. Another friend came all the way from Vietnam, came wearing his uniform, came to the hospital before he went home to see his family.

Other friends drove all the way from Washington, D. C.—went hours out of their way to stop by my house and pick up my favorite Picasso print so my hospital room could look more like home. The doctor himself sent in a woman who had been similarly injured, and who was now perfectly healthy, to prove that total healing was possible.

I introduced everyone to my friend who had taught me to drive, who had tried to sit calmly in the passenger seat as I drove his new Rover 2000 TC around the track at the high school. He, too, shared stories from his life.

All of these people thought of *me* as their teacher, and I thought of them as *mine*. All of them were open and trusting and eager, all of them listened the way you listen when you really do want to understand something, when you have no impulse to interrupt, to talk for the sake of talking, to talk in order to show off, to prove, or disprove.

Why couldn't my classes be like this? What could I do to help break through the barriers that prevented such goodness from happening? That's what I wanted to learn, more than anything.

THAT'S THE BREAKS

The car accident occurred on May 18, 1969. I was released from the hospital August 8. Fall classes began the last week of August, before Labor Day. On my birthday, September 25, 1969, there was a letter in my mailbox that told me my contract with the college was not being renewed, and that therefore my tenure with that institution would be over at the end of the current academic year. I read the letter twice. That's what it said. "How could this be—when not a word was said about my job being in jeopardy, when, in fact, I was specifically informed that it was not?" I asked an administrator. He said that if I had enrolled in a Ph.D. program during the summer my job would have been secure. "But you know that I was in a body cast in the hospital for all but the last two weeks!" I said. He shrugged his shoulders. "That's the breaks," he said, and walked away.

I didn't know things like this happened. I didn't know what I should do about it. There was no faculty union. No appeal process was mentioned in the letter. I would be on crutches for the rest of the semester. Over Christmas, I would have surgery to remove the pin from my leg. I had medical bills that insurance had not covered. I had no car, and was not yet able to drive. What should I do? I decided to appeal anyway—offer to enter a Ph.D. program the following summer. Not soon enough, was the reply. I would have to begin a Ph.D. program as soon as I could be admitted to one. I applied, was given permission to begin in January, a week after my surgery, took out a loan for the tuition, bought an old Volvo 544. Over the next nine years, I took out nine loans, one a year, spent many more years paying them back, and completed the degree in 1979.

I described my Ph.D. classes to my students, and explained how I happened to enroll in the Ph.D. program, told them that, until now, I had always loved school, loved reading, loved discussing, loved learning. Now, I said, it was painful, discouraging. It was not something I had freely chosen, not something I would have wanted. I didn't know how I could put my heart into it under these circumstances. I wondered how I was going to afford it, how I could possibly have a *life* for the next nine years. I asked them, "Is it like that for you, too? Is it discouraging and painful for you, too? Or is it a pleasure, being a student?"

They looked at me in startled, uncomfortable silence. I waited. A few giggled, glanced around the room to see if anyone was going to say something. They looked at their desks, studied their hands in their laps. "I mean it," I said. "I really want to know. I don't see how I can teach you anything worthwhile unless I know—because I don't want to cause *you* pain." Still, silence. I waited longer.

Finally, a boy in the back raised his hand. The rest of the class turned to look at him. "This is the third time I've taken this class," he said. "I've failed it twice. I'm a senior. I don't know how I'll ever pass. It's *pain!*" A few laughed. A girl said she went to a Catholic school where a nun hit her fingers with a ruler every time she spelled a word wrong.

A boy said that in elementary school, a teacher with thick red lipstick humiliated the boys who made spelling, grammar, and punctuation errors by sending them into the coat closet and kissing them there. He said they came out with bright red faces and bright red lipstick on their cheeks. He had dreaded English ever since.

By now, all the students were grinning, laughing, raising their hands. They told me how their teachers pointed out their errors in front of the entire class, made them read their papers aloud when they knew they were poor readers. They described how their papers were "torn apart," covered with red ink. Even now, they said, they were always criticized, never praised for anything. Even fellow students made fun of them if they earned a low grade. They said they always had to write what the teacher would like, and not what they had to say. They were never allowed to develop their own style. Sometimes, they were not even allowed to have opinions—unless the teacher shared them. If a teacher was a Christian, someone said, then Christian students got A's. You couldn't use "I" in a sentence. You couldn't swear. You had to write everything in third person. Who could sound real in third person?

They said teachers didn't care what they had to say, as long as they had a proper thesis sentence, as long as their papers were organized, as long as they used correct grammar and spelling. They said English was boring; English was a waste of time. English was impossible to learn. They believed you could write—or you couldn't; you were creative—or uncreative. English should be like football. Not everybody can play football. Football is not required of everyone. Why take a course you can't improve in? What meaning could a grade have, if you just give teachers what they want to hear? If they had writing talent, wouldn't it have been discovered by now?

I never realized, I said. Until I started the Ph.D. program and saw how stuffy and dull and pretentious some of the professors were, how impressed they were with themselves, I never realized. But how could we turn so much negativity around? What could I do that might help? What could we all do? And if these were the pains students associated with school, with English, then what might be the pleasures? *Were* there any pleasures, for students—other than passing the course and putting it behind them?

That semester, and many others, there were no pleasures that students knew of, at the beginning. But, they said, there might be. It might be a pleasure to write—if they didn't have to worry about mechanics, if I marked spelling, grammar, and punctuation errors, but didn't grade on them. It might be a pleasure—if they could revise their papers for a grade. It might help if I just listened when they expressed their opinions, and didn't argue with them, if I gave them suggestions for writing subjects, but still allowed them to write about something else, if they wished.

I could easily do these things, I said. And I knew of a way to improve mechanics that was almost painless, that was even fun. All it required was a commitment from them to appear in my office as soon as papers were handed back, to sit down with me, and list their most common errors, so that, together, we could analyze their "system" of spelling and punctuating. Once I understood theirs, I said, I could show them how to understand mine. I told them that, the previous semester, one student had made over a hundred errors in a paper; by the end, he was making only four or five, even in his term paper. There was hope for them. As for worries that they were not free to disagree with me, I said, they could forget them. I really did understand that their ideas grew out of their lives as my ideas grew out of mine. I loved teaching composition because no two students were alike. Even identical twins had different ideas and different writing styles. I loved finding out how people came to have their ideas. I understood that grades caused many people pain. I was not free to eliminate them, but they were welcome to discuss their rough drafts with me, and to rewrite papers, and I would even consider giving them an opportunity to evaluate and grade their own work sometimes. Of course, we would not always have the same views of their work. I valued honesty, thoughtfulness, thoroughness, clarity, and a reasonable amount of mechanical correctness. Writers themselves might have other concerns—because, after all, they see and feel and know the writing from the inside. The reader knows only what he or she hears. They cannot always be the same.

"LITERARY GENERAL"

The first day of class, there were seven students in our small circle—one boy, six anemic, academic girls. The second day of class, there were more than thirty fraternity brothers of the first boy. They had arranged their chairs in a circle around the periphery of the room. It was a huge room, a huge circle.

The class was called Literary Genres, a sophomore-level General Education course for non-majors, as we called them. These new ones referred to it as "Literary General." They didn't know the word "genres," and didn't care what it meant. The brothers had always wanted to take a course together. This, they told me, was their opportunity. They laughed defiantly, dared me to challenge them.

I always brought my camera to class the first week. I took everyone's picture, learned one hundred ten names and faces this way. I waved it in the air, as threateningly as I could, walked around the circle slowly, leaned close to each brother, looked each in the eye, told each I expected to see him in that exact seat every day of the semester, with his assignment read, ready to speak his mind—no excuses, no "my ride left early," no "my grandmother died three or four times during the semester," no "I partied too late," no "I had to study for a test in another class," no nothing. They grinned at me. I grinned back. I was not afraid of students like these now. I liked them. I liked their frankness, their lack of pretense, their—I almost want to say—innocence.

I asked these students to write me a note about what mattered in their lives, about what was worth thinking about, worth remembering—told them I would build the course around whatever they wrote there, if it was sincere. I told them we would begin, the next day, by discussing a poem they couldn't stand, asked each of them to supply such a poem, make their contribution the absolute worst they could find. We would try to determine what it was that made a bad poem bad. I asked them to draw a picture of themselves doing something they would rather be doing than attending a Literary General class. They all drew stick figures playing baseball, drinking beer, watching television, sleeping. I asked for such a drawing every semester for the next twenty-some years. These are the drawings everyone made, even English majors.

They told me that what mattered was making their parents proud of them, becoming good parents themselves someday, getting a good job, an interesting job, making good money, having a good life. We discussed what good parents, good jobs, good lives were, and were not. We discussed their poems—all of them "old," "flowery," too ornate and indirect for them. We read them as mockingly as we could, laughed at them, criticized them, got those poems out of their systems. We "translated" a few of them. They were relieved to learn that they didn't have to like them, to learn that all poems couldn't possibly be accessible to all people, to learn that it was our living that determined what it was that would be accessible to us—that, and a talent for "translating"—which, they were willing to concede now, might be a talent they could learn.

I asked them to bring a favorite children's story to the next class meeting. If they themselves had no favorite, I told them, call up a friend, ask for a recommendation, plan to read their selection aloud. They did that, came the next time with thirty stories, read them in small groups, remembered or discovered what a pleasure it was to read for the fun of it, to notice anything they wished, to let the story take them wherever it could. We discussed the themes and the characters of these stories. We discussed what made a good children's story.

I brought in my copies of Richard Lewis's books: *Miracles* and *Journeys*, poems and stories written by English-speaking children around the world, read them aloud for an entire class meeting. Some students wiped tears from their eyes; some laughed. They couldn't believe that children could think like that, could have imaginations like that, could be so honest about such important things, could show such sensitivity, such compassion. "What if *we*, ourselves, could have written like this?" I asked. "What if our schools, our teachers, had been different? What if they had respected our minds, and welcomed what was unique about us?"

It was wonderful to meet a group of students like these, who were "just themselves," who didn't pretend to know what they didn't know, or pretend not to know what they did know. It was a pleasure to be trusted with who they were, to be allowed to remodel their understanding of what literature was, what a literature class was.

Prior to this class, I had felt immensely sad, had felt my biological clock ticking, had wished I could have found a way to put aside doctoral work, find a man, settle down, raise a family, be as I supposed others were, be part of a family of choice. Though I didn't want to, I had made a commitment to complete the Ph.D. program in order to keep my job, which I did want. I didn't know any alternatives. I assumed that to teach elsewhere I would need the degree too. I had given this as much thought as I had been able to give it and had decided to hope that it would be enough to borrow other people's children, to do my best to accept them as they were, celebrate them, stretch them, share my present moments with them, as festively as I could, so that the moments we

were together felt positive, added up to something both they and I considered worth our while.

I had told myself that there were already millions of unhappy children in the world who could use an addition of something positive in
their lives, had said that it didn't matter whether I added something
large or something small. After all, I, myself, was small, as Frost says,
"measured against the All" (Frost 1949, 366). I would add what I could
add, do my best not to take anything valuable away. I would hope that,
when it came time for me to decide, I would be able to say to myself
that this was a gift of sufficient value, both for me and for the young
people whose lives I touched, that it would do enough to soften the
edges of my disappointment at not having been able to welcome my
own children into the world.

CLUES

> "To have insight into the child's strivings and the problems he
> faces, the teacher must strive to face the same problems within his
> own life. These problems are largely emotional in nature."
>
> Arthur T. Jersild, *When Teachers Face Themselves*

Every year, several faculty members at my institution were invited to
participate in an introductory mini-course program at a remote high
school in the northern part of the state, so that the students there could
have some idea what it might be like to go on to college. I volunteered
every year. It was a pleasure to go there, to visit with an administrator
who took risks, who, in his fifties, had decided that he could not go on
teaching and administering in the traditional ways he had been accustomed to all his life. I liked the way he talked, the way he was with children, the way he noticed what I did in the classroom, the way he remembered, from one visit to the next, what we discussed. I liked his
students. They were eager learners—quick with questions, willing to
try approaches they hadn't been exposed to before, comfortable with
the way their minds worked, supportive of each other.

It occurred to me that I might visit students in other classes, other
grades, in this school district, ask questions, compare answers. I had

been reading Arthur T. Jersild's *When Teachers Face Themselves* (1955) and *In Search of Self* (1952), and found his insights concerning students' and teachers' anxiety, loneliness, anger, and compassion particularly helpful and encouraging. I was eager to find some ways to address these areas with my college students, to understand, better than I did, how they might have developed their present dread of reading and writing, and how their schooling might have affected their self-confidence and self-esteem, or lack of it. In my youth, I had taught swimming to children who were afraid of the water and had been able to empathize with their fears and help them overcome them. It seemed to me that fear of academic courses might be quite similar. If I observed and listened to younger children, children I was not responsible for, children I did not have to evaluate for a grade, I might find it easier to earn their trust and might, by sharing what I learned from them, deepen the trust of my college students as well.

That semester, I visited elementary, middle, and high school classes in three counties, first to observe, and then to ask students to write about some of the things that concerned them most. I was surprised to discover that these students, unlike my college students, were eager to talk to a stranger about their lives. They answered my questions willingly, and, especially at the high school level, wrote at length about how difficult it was for them to talk with their families, and even their friends, and how stressful and unhappy their lives were.

After half a dozen visits to these schools, I realized that it didn't matter very much where I went or what age level the students were. All of them seemed to long for someone who would just listen to them without criticizing and judging them. They were very aware of the many ways in which they could be rejected, by their families, their teachers, and especially their peers, and they realized how, so often, they also criticized and rejected themselves. Rejection, it was clear, wherever it came from, was never something you could forget about for long. It was frightening to anticipate and difficult to get over.

When an elementary principal invited me to visit a third grade class for a year, I was delighted. Somehow, in spite of everything I was learning elsewhere, I assumed that *high school* would be the most painful time for most students. I had not yet allowed myself to realize that third grade might be a terrible time too. When the third grade teacher agreed to allow me to take over the class as often as every two weeks to teach whatever lesson I might devise, and said I might talk with the children individually or in small groups whenever they had finished their regular lessons, and might sit among the students, and watch and listen to everything that went on, and take notes on whatever I wished, I was not suspicious of her motives. I rejoiced in my good fortune and could hardly wait for my second year in third grade to begin.

SEEING

> "What does one person give to another? He gives of himself, of the most precious he has, he gives of his life. This does not necessarily mean that he sacrifices his life for the other—but that he gives him of that which is alive in him; he gives him of his joy, of his interest, of his understanding, of his knowledge, of his humor, of his sadness—of all expressions and manifestations of that which is alive in him. In thus giving of his life, he enriches the other person, he enhances the other's sense of aliveness by enhancing his own sense of aliveness. He does not give in order to receive; giving is, in itself, exquisite joy. But in giving he cannot help bringing something to life in the other person, and this which is brought to life reflects back to him; in truly giving, he cannot help receiving that which is given back to him."
>
> Erich Fromm, *The Art of Loving*

What I expected to see in third grade was not what was there to see. I realized that as soon as I had taken off my coat and squeezed myself into one of the tiny chairs a row away from the window that looked out on the concrete playground. It was a grimly quiet room. All eyes faced forward. All students sat stiffly, in total silence.

The girl behind me leaned close to me, whispered that her name was Katherine. I turned, smiled at her, whispered hi, told her my name. Mrs. Marshall, in the midst of a lesson on abbreviations, didn't introduce me to the class and went on with the lesson, following instructions in the Teacher's Guide, asking questions the guide said she should ask, rolling her eyes when students answered incorrectly or when they didn't answer at all. She told them they were the gifted class, but they weren't nearly as smart as they thought they were. The children took this in silence, did not protest, did not laugh, did not turn around or lean over to remark on her judgment to their neighbors.

I felt as if I had heard something that I was not supposed to hear, felt ashamed to see that this was how she saw them, judged them, found them wanting. I wondered how she could value this stiff, unnatural, fearful silence. I wondered how it was that she couldn't tolerate spontaneity and noise and playfulness, how it had happened that she was not spontaneous and playful herself, how it was that she had decided to put abbreviations on such a pedestal. I wondered why abbreviations couldn't be fun—for her and for them.

Mrs. Marshall asked what abbreviations were for, and, answering her own question, said we had abbreviations because we were all lazy. People were often forgetful too, she added, instructing the boy who had just written his initials on the board to supply periods. She asked how many months there were, raised her voice, directed her remark at me, said, rolling her eyes, that one student in this class thought there were twenty-four months. Two students frowned, waved their arms in the air, and asked what to do with June.

She instructed the students to write their own initials on scratch paper and checked to see that they had completed this task correctly. As she leaned over to look at a student's paper, she remarked, with a sigh, "You people are just not creative, even if you *are* the top section!" When she reached me, she said, disgust clear in her voice, "I usually like this class, but there is one boy that I can't stand. Every composition he writes, every book he reads, every drawing he draws, is about *sharks*."

"Really!?" I asked. "You mean he knows enough about sharks to keep writing without repeating himself? I wish my college students could do that! I'd like to meet a student like that!"

She invited me to follow her. A boy looked up and grinned when he saw we were headed his way. She rested her hand on his head, roughed up his hair, spoke with nothing but irritation in her voice:

"This is Alex. He has a one-track mind. All he ever thinks about is sharks," she said, then turned and walked toward her desk.

Alex lowered his head, embarrassed, dismayed. I knelt down next to him, bent down far enough so that I had to look up to see his eyes.

"Hey, Alex," I whispered. "That's *great* that you know so much about sharks at your age!"

In a few seconds, he sat up straight, whispered that he would like to be "an oceanographer, like Jacques Cousteau" when he grew up.

Ellie, a shy, quiet girl across the aisle from him, had been listening. She leaned across the aisle, and whispered that Mrs. Marshall thought *she* had a one-track mind too, because she always wanted to write about her mother.

"Why is that?" I whispered back.

It was because her mother had died when she was in first grade.

I was so surprised that tears filled my eyes.

"Ellie," I said. "I'll be back every Monday and Friday all year, and it will be fine if you write about your mother for me."

I wrote down my telephone number and handed it to her, told her she was welcome to call if she ever felt lonely and just wanted to talk to somebody. She thanked me, and slipped the piece of paper into her purse.

I remained in the empty room after the class was over and asked, as nonchalantly as I could, how it was that Mrs. Marshall had decided to become a teacher.

"Because I love kids," she said. "It's just that I want these kids to follow my rules. They're not used to rules. They had too much freedom in second grade. They're spoiled."

She said it was hard to teach the top class because they all had minds of their own. She wished they were more docile and compliant, like the children in her other sections. She worked hard to encourage them to write about uninteresting things, because that was what school was about, and that had always been hard for her when she was a child. She just couldn't get them to put aside their interests.

There was a lot of pressure on her, she said. She had to try to please the teachers who would have these students in fourth grade, and she had to try to please their parents. There was always someone to please, and pleasing them all was impossible. In theory, she was free to use any textbooks she wished, but how could she exercise her so-called freedom under these circumstances? She chose the texts she did to please all those who needed pleasing. To choose according to her interests—that would be too risky. But to choose against her interests made her life miserable.

REMEMBERING THE PLEASURE OF IT

I had decided that the first thing I wanted to convey to all these children was that I would enjoy hearing what each one had to say about something that was easy and fun to talk about. I wanted to be as sure as possible that my first exercise threatened no one, caused no one pain. I explained this to Mrs. Marshall, and said I would like to begin with a Kenneth Koch exercise about wishes (*Wishes, Lies, and Dreams* 1970, 56–65). I would like to bring my typewriter to class, and sit down with it in the middle of the room. After all the children had written one wish, I would like each person to walk over to me and read his or her sentence aloud so I could type it into one huge list of wishes. I didn't want to stand up during this exercise. I wanted to be on the children's eye level.

Mrs. Marshall assured me that this was fine, even offered to have a student take my typed paper to the office when we were finished and duplicate it so we could distribute a copy to each child that same day.

The next Friday I arrived with my typewriter. Kids crowded around me, asking what we were going to do. They couldn't believe I was going to "do something." For weeks now I had always been seated with them. I had always spoken in whispers, as they had. And now here I was, standing up, looking official, carrying a typewriter.

I told them I would be taking over the class every once in a while from now on, doing what I called "experiments." In all of these experiments, they would be free to say whatever they wished. There would be no wrong answers. They could spell however they wished, could ask anyone they wished for help with spelling, could look words up in their dictionaries if they wanted to. The papers would not be graded. They would not be shown to any adult they knew, or to any other child. I would take their writings home, put them in a box under my bed, and get them out again many years later, after they had grown up, after they had forgotten all about them, and put them in a book about how it felt to be a kid, in school, in third grade.

"You mean you won't show them to Mrs. Marshall?" someone asked.

"That's right."

"You won't show them to our parents?"

"I won't."

The room grew suddenly quiet. One boy asked, cautiously, slowly, as if he were just waking up from a long sleep: "Can we—*swear*?????" There was not a sound. All eyes were on me.

I had not anticipated this question. "Hm-m-m," I said. "I need to think about this one."

They sat in absolute silence, allowing me all the time I needed. No one laughed. No one called out. No one said anything. No one moved. An image of myself at approximately their age slipped into view. I was walking home from the elementary school, past the natatorium, past the tennis courts. I was whispering "Shit, shit, shit" under my breath. I wasn't angry. I wasn't shocked. I wasn't scared. I wasn't responding to anything. I was just trying out the word, seeing what it felt like to say it. I knew, for certain, that if I ever said it more audibly in the presence of adults, especially in the presence of my father, I would be "beaten within an inch of my life."

Another image came into view, this time of my father heatedly saying "Horse manure!" when he disagreed with us. I had no idea how long this little reverie lasted.

"Well," I said, slowly. "It seems to me that what comes out of your mouth belongs to *you*, so *you* should be the one to decide whether to swear or not. But I'll tell you now that whether you swear or not, what I'll be doing is trying to understand what you're writing to me about in the first place. I'll be looking *through* the swearing to find that. I might not even notice the swearing."

All the kids cheered, applauded, laughed. "All *right*!!!!" someone said. "All *right*!!!!"

Not one student swore in this first exercise. Their wishes were simple, direct, diverse. They wrote their sentences, skipped, sauntered, strolled, cavorted up to me, told me confidently, shyly, eagerly, hesitantly, that they wanted to be hammerhead sharks, gazelles, a fawn half an inch tall, a roaring tiger, a kitten, a princess. Sandra hid under her desk, peeked out at me, couldn't think of what she wanted to be. Those around her called out suggestions: "Be a horse! Be Jaws! Be a deer!" She decided she wanted to be an Indian maiden, crawled out from the desk, wrote, read her paper to me, grinning happily: "I want to be an Indian maiden." She turned, giggled at her friends, and returned to her seat.

When the papers came back, they read through them. "Oh, I know who *that* is!" they said. "That's Alex." "That's Ann-Marie." "That's Ron. That's—Oh, look! A fawn half an inch tall. I wonder who wrote *that?*"

A few weeks later, we did another exercise. They had been laboriously, dutifully, making vocabulary lists on 3 × 5 cards: A words, B words, C words, filling the cards, trying to avoid the "itsy-bitsy" words that Mrs. Marshall always criticized. I brought in bright orange and blue 5 × 8 cards, asked them to write on one side, "What I Like," on the other, "What I Don't Like." I told them not to worry about spelling. They wrote "tuna surprise," "broccoli," "cauliflower," "vacations," "summer," "Jessica," "Ron," "Mrs. Marshall," "pizza," "The Steelers," "riding my bike," "riding my horse," "fishing." They filled their cards on both sides, came up to me, read their lists aloud, read them aloud to each other.

Mrs. Marshall assigned endless worksheets. I decided, next, to imitate worksheets, design "blanks with a difference," change them week after week. They never grew tired of them. Some of them filled all these blanks, some only a few lines. Occasionally, someone simply signed her name to show me she was present, as I had asked her to do. Some asked for "my papers" back every day I came so they could add to them.

Sometimes, I borrowed the format for my exercise from poems Richard Lewis had collected (Lewis, *Miracles* 1966, 38, 136), leaving large spaces blank: "Grown-ups are blank. They never blank when blank. They just blank. Isn't that blank?" Usually, I just invented blanks and tried to anticipate how the third graders might fill them: "I wish blank. Then I would blank. I would blank until blank. Then I would blank." "Sometimes I think blank. And I think blank. But mostly I think blank."

They read their answers aloud to me, read them aloud to their friends, fell back on their desks, shook with laughter. Happy, relieved tears ran down their cheeks.

When I arrived now, half a dozen hands waved in the air; half a dozen voices called out, "Sit by me! Sit by me!" When I stood near them, they leaned against me, hugged me, showed me the books they were reading, told me what their parents were doing with their income tax refund, announced that their grandfather had died, explained how their parents responded to that news, informed me where they were going after school, commented that they had just gotten back from Disneyworld, asked if this was a mood ring I was wearing, wondered if I was passionate, said they saw me walking my dog on Market Street yesterday, last night, this morning, said that they saw me jogging past their house at exactly seven-fifteen and that their mom and dad told time by me in the morning, told me they had buried a treasure down by the river, they had fallen off their bikes, they had started baseball season, they had tried to count to infinity, they had gotten in trouble for talking, for forgetting their homework, for looking out the window.

When I sat down, they ran their fingers through my hair, restyled it, piled it on top of my head, thought it looked better that way, borrowed my coat and scarf, wore them the rest of the period, passed my hat and gloves around the room, tried them on, pretended they wouldn't ever let me have them back, stood on my left, poked me on my right arm, pretended someone else did it, told me I was a foggy person, said I was the silliest person they had ever met, and that if I thought I had a sense of humor, I was mistaken. They called me Mrs. Magillacutty, wrote rhymes about me, sang me songs, gave me suggestions for "my papers," asked me if I was going out this Friday night, told me where they were going.

In a few months, third grade was a whole new place as soon as I opened the door, and the third graders were whole new people. They had their natural buoyancy back. The weight of much of their anger and fear was gone. They still *felt* anger and fear, and had a huge backlog of those emotions and others, but they realized that talking and writing about their emotional lives with someone they trusted helped them to endure them and to put them in perspective.

SOMETIMES I WISH

Sometimes I wish I had a pet monkey.
And sometimes I wish I had a lion.
Sometimes I wish I had a boyfriend.
And I wish that I was never born.
And I wish my Dad was a movey star.
But mostly I wish I could have a Mom.

Grown-ups are bosie
They never listen to you

when you talk.
They just egnour you.

Grown-ups are mean.
They never take time
when we want them to.
They just yell, yell, yell.
Isn't that domb?

Grown-ups are dumb.
They never think you know anything.
When you want to go out you can't.
They just are mean
And have a bad temper.

Grown-ups are over-tempered.
They never care for us.
My dad just sits and drinks beer
and waces football games
and sits in his favorite chair
and eats potato chips while my mother
is working like crazy.
I think that's retarted.

Grown-ups are bose.
They never look right
when there green.
They just sit there
and snort
until they turn red.
Isn't that a terrabel sight?

Once there was a magic star.
It lived out in the sky.
It lived in the sky and liked it there.
So it was happy
until it disapered.
And then there was never one again.

Once there was a magic tree.
It lived out in the woods.

It lived in the woods and forst.
So it truned things blue
until the sun came up.
And then it melted.

MY LIFE OF CRIME

Nathan wrote a paragraph for me about the time he got in trouble for stealing candy at the grocery store on a shopping trip with his parents. He told me how excited he had been to get at the candy, how he had hurried out of the store, climbed into the car, and started eating, as his parents, without realizing what he had done, loaded the groceries into the trunk. Suddenly, they heard the crinkling of a candy wrapper, knew they hadn't bought him any candy, asked him where the candy had come from. He told them. They made him go back into the store and apologize to the manager. He called his paragraph, "My Life of Crime."

I sat in my car outside the elementary school reading his paragraph, wondering how I might respond to it, remembering a line from Edgar Lee Masters's *Spoon River Anthology* about a boy who had stolen an apple and who had then gone on to steal larger things, until he did, indeed, have "a life of crime." It's how we "regard the theft of the apple that makes a boy what he is," the poem says (Masters 1962, 77). I decided that, just to be on the safe side, I would like to see if I could alter the way Nathan was looking at himself. I had no idea how to accomplish this. Never having been a parent myself, I didn't know what goes through parents' minds when they find their children doing unacceptable things like this, but I remembered well how my friend in first or second grade had been accused of stealing, and how I, though I had never seen her take anything, had been questioned by the principal and then ordered by my father not to walk home with that little girl anymore. I remembered, too, how one of my siblings, at the age of five or six, or younger, had been beaten for taking change from our father's dresser. I figured just about any affirmative message would have better results than such thoughtless and insensitive attacks on children's character.

I drove the remaining few blocks to town, parked the car, and began gathering samples of hard candy from just about every store on Main Street that sold candy. Half an hour later, I had a bag of individually wrapped candy about the size of a ten-pound bag of cat litter. I drove to the store where Nathan said he had stolen the candy, asked for a grocery bag, put the other bag in that one, wrapped the entire package in white tissue paper, and tied it with a wide red ribbon, as if it were a Christmas present. The next day, I called Nathan over while the rest of the class was working, whispered that it was for him, told him I had put a note inside explaining it, and suggested that he not open it until after the class was over. He looked at me solemnly and agreed to that. My note said: "Since you have experience in this territory, I decided that you should be the keeper of the goods." I put the bag in his lap, grinned at him, and sat down in another part of the room.

That evening, I received a call from his mother: "Our son says that you gave him this huge bag of candy. Is that true?" "Yes," I said. "It is." She asked what he was supposed to do with it. I told her he could do whatever he wished.

About two weeks later, two of the shyest boys in the class looked at each other, rose from their seats at the same time, and walked toward me, in an unmistakably purposeful way, their heads much higher than usual. They stood next to me in silence for a minute, then one of them spoke. "Nathan ate *all* the candy," he said. "And *we* think that *we* should have been the keepers of the goods, because *we* have experience in the territory *too!*" This caught me by surprise. My first impulse was to laugh, but I looked away for a second, stifled it, and turned back to them. "Goodness!" I said. "I *never* thought that would happen! I thought he would share it with the class! I see that I'll have to give this some thought. Give me a few days, and I will send you both a note." They thanked me, solemnly, and returned to their seats.

The identical notes I handed to each of them a few days later said this: "I am sorry to learn that Nathan ate all the candy, but, since you have experience in the territory, I am sure that you have many other talents as well, and *one* of them *must* be making chocolate chip cookies. So, if it's okay with your parents, show up at my front door on Wednesday after school, and we'll make so many chocolate chip cookies that there will be enough for everyone in class, and you two can eat all those that are left over!"

They opened the envelopes and read the notes without so much as a glance in my direction. On Wednesday, two small, beaming boys knocked at my door, and we began the first of a two-year, all boys, chocolate chip cookie-making tradition. I found stools for each of them to stand on, so they could reach my kitchen counter. I read them the directions; they measured the flour, sugar, salt, baking soda, shortening, vanilla, and chocolate chips into the bowl, and took turns stirring, until their arms were tired, then I finished the mixing. We greased the pans, and they excitedly dipped out over a hundred cookies, carefully lined them up in the pans, and watched through the oven window as the cookies spread out and browned. They introduced themselves to my cats—Mouse, Muffin, Rats, Pooh, and Piglet—and to Hede, my collie shepherd, and talked about their day at school, and, every few minutes, they ran into the kitchen, bent down by the oven, and peered in to see how the cookies were doing. When the timer went off, I gave them pot holders, and they carefully carried the cookie sheets to the table, grinning, talking excitedly about how surprised the class would be tomorrow when they came in with a treat for everyone that they had made themselves. When the cookies cooled, we divided them into three bags: one for the class, and one for each of them. Their classmates and their teacher all agreed that the cookies were *great*.

The next year, half a dozen boys, including Nathan and these two, approached me, asked if we could make some more chocolate chip cookies. We did. This time, we finished with a giant cookie that filled the cookie pan and somehow caused the pan to rise up on one side in the oven until it was at least an inch in the air. We all marveled at this, couldn't explain it, didn't try. When it was done, we flipped it over and flipped it again into a special box marked with the teacher's name.

Everyone believed that fairness had been achieved at last, and, I hope, learned that a little compassion for ourselves never hurt anything, and sometimes was a lot of fun as well. And I have not spent a minute, in the last twenty-five years, worrying that any of these boys might some day have to write a longer, and more painful essay, about his life of crime.

RHODODENDRON

As a ninth grader, I was the winner of our junior high school spelling bee because I could spell "rhododendron" and the runner-up couldn't. I studied for this test by reading the dictionary, starting with the A's and moving on to the B's. I never got to the R's. I don't know how it was that I could spell "rhododendron."

I *like* words, have liked words ever since I was old enough to understand that my grandparents were all immigrants, that they all spoke with an "accent." I wanted to speak with an "accent" too—say "Yingle bells" and "Yule kaka" and "tack så mycket" and "var så god." In elementary school, I was proud to be able to count to ten, and then to twenty, in Swedish, am delighted, even now, when, in Europe and in the United States, I am mistaken, every once in a while, for a Canadian.

I have always loved books—not just for the content, but for the physical thing that a book is—for its rough or smooth pages, for its type style, its illustrations, its smell, its weight, its colors. It was a privilege, as a child, to search through the heavy, thumb-indexed family dictionary for the word I needed, to read words before and after and next to the word, to come across the dried roses my mother was in the habit of saving there.

I collect dictionaries—and phrase books—from many countries, have dozens upon dozens of them. I voluntarily enrolled in a year of Anglo-Saxon, delighted in what seemed to be its similarity to Swedish, and I teach those lovely, heavy, unsubtle words, even now, to the elementary students I tutor—so they can know that words are fun, that words are useful, that words make sense, that words come in historical and even political contexts, that words change, that spelling is not a matter of "rules" after all, that "rules" are really exceptions to the exceptions, that there is nothing permanent about them, nothing, that is, worth losing your confidence and your self-esteem over.

I introduced the fun of words to my college students by bringing boxes of my dictionaries to class, arranging students in small groups, handing them dictionaries, and asking them to make a list of "emergency vocabulary" that might be useful if they were to travel to another country for business or pleasure. I told them they could put anything they wished on their list, offered to invite members of the community who spoke those languages to visit us, give us a lesson in pronunciation, answer any questions we might have.

What a pleasure it was to hear them laugh, to see them trying to pronounce words, to see them reading dictionaries to each other.

If they seemed embarrassed about their spelling at the beginning, I gave them my best imitation of public school. I announced that we would have a "spelling test." They groaned, sighed, reached into their backpacks for paper. I gave them these words: a lot, already, all right, their, they're, there, to, too, believe, receive, definitely, prejudiced, sophomore, weird, genealogy, and Volkswagen, and told them these were the most commonly misspelled words in all my college classes.

They laughed. "This is a piece of cake," they said. They *knew* these words. They wouldn't be like my other students. They wouldn't miss any of *these*. I knew better. I told them to *cheat*, to copy from each other, write answers on the soles of their shoes, cross their legs at the knee, write on their fingernails, pass notes. They said they didn't need these suggestions—until they got to "genealogy" and "Volkswagen." They eagerly volunteered to spell these words correctly as we marked their papers.

"No!" half the class said, on "a lot." "It's not two words! It's *one* word!" They offered to go to the library, check an unabridged dictionary. I let them go. The library was right next door. They came back, incredulous. "It *is*, you guys. It *is*! It's *two words*! I never knew that!" They did the same for almost every word on the list, thought "already" and "all right" must follow a rule, spelled them both with one *l*. Half the class left out the middle *o* in "sophomore," had *dj* instead of *j* in "prejudiced," omitted the second *e* in "definitely," got their *i*'s and *e*'s mixed up, had no idea how to spell "weird," didn't know the entire "*i* before *e*" rhyme, took wild guesses on "genealogy" and "Volkswagen." Some said they drove Volkswagens and certainly knew how to spell the name of their own car! They never thought of "gen." Some threatened to drive all the way to the Volkswagen dealership in the next town to prove they were right.

What a liberating exercise this was for them every semester. Until this "test," they believed that they were not college material, that they would never become good writers, that writers were born, not made. And then they saw that virtually all of their classmates felt exactly as they did, saw that they never suspected that perfectly ordinary words were the culprits, never suspected that they didn't know how to spell them because they were all taught spelling in third, fourth, and fifth grade, in the same meaningless and confusing way everyone else had been taught, in the same way the local third graders were being taught decades later. It was as if a huge burden had leaped off their shoulders, and galloped out the door. Think of it! They were not dumb! They were not hopeless! I hadn't given them very many words. They could easily memorize these—or just keep a list of them in their notebooks, check their list after they wrote each paper for the class, add a few words to their list every week. Maybe, after all, writing *was* about having something to say! Maybe it *was* about really listening to what others said! It was worth a try; it was worth a try!

The third graders were not so hopeful. In third grade, words were grim business, spelling was something to have a test over, workbooks were something to be graded on, dialogue was a word that ended in "gue" and that must be used in a sentence. That sentence must not be too short, must not offend the teacher, must be copied over in one's best penmanship and turned in. In third grade, words were part of a never-ending performance, test, and time-filler. Words were nonsense. Words were work for which you did not get paid—ever.

Third grade spelling words were never chosen by students, were always on the board on Monday, to be copied, used in sentences and paragraphs, memorized by acts of will. Third grade spelling words were never chosen for their meaning—they were chosen because they illustrated "rules." They came without meaningful contexts—had to be stretched and strained to fit life as an eight-year-old knew it. This stretching was work, was tedium, was unending stress. When given a chance to write freely, about whatever they wished, third graders rarely used *any* of these words.

WHAT DID YOU LEARN IN SCHOOL TODAY?

> Teacher: What's this? What's that? How is this? How is that?
> Student: Who cares?
>> Conversation during "Reading Comprehension"

The best way to understand third graders is to become a spy there—not to hide in the coat closet or under the radiator or behind the teacher's desk, but to sit in one of the small seats that you can barely squeeze your adult body into, so your eyes and ears are near the eyes and ears of eight-year-olds, and then watch, and listen.

What you will see and hear there, when you are perceived as "someone on their level," will, at the very least, astound and sadden you, not because of what the children are, but because of what teaching is, or, in many classrooms, has become.

It has become, first, a battle, not for the minds and hearts of children, but for their spirits—not to enrich them, not to inspire them, not to love them, not to nurture them, but to destroy them totally. Don't tell me I am exaggerating. Don't say this could not possibly be. Go there, and watch, and listen, and make that discovery for yourself. Go twice a week for a year. Go twice a week, or more, for ten years, for fourteen, eighteen, twenty-two. Go there until you are so emotionally drained yourself that you simply cannot go there anymore. And then write the story of what you saw and heard. Unless many miracles happen between that time and this, you will see and hear what I have seen and heard, and you will feel as I have felt about it.

You will see, in third grade, that brilliant children, the brightest the school has, are told constantly to shut up, to turn around, to sit still, to copy spelling words, to memorize spelling words, to use spelling words in sentences that make no sense to third graders, who are all Anglo-Saxon in their raw energy, in their hunger for hair-raising, spine-tingling adventure, in their inability to hold their hands and legs and mouths still. You will see that these same calfish and coltish creatures must spend time every day in reading groups, reading graded readers filled with poems that are not real poems and stories that are ten thousand times less imaginative than the least imaginative eight-year-old on his or her worst day. And then you will see the teacher throwing a choke chain around each of their necks and unceremoniously jerking a dozen of them at once into a circle around her and her graded reader teacher's guide to see if they have "comprehended" these same stories and poems that were not worth comprehending in the first place.

You will see that every day in third grade, unless there is a fire drill or an earthquake, or an in-service day. And then you will see it in fourth grade, and fifth, and sixth, and on and on, until you yourself never want to see a graded reader, or hear a "discussion" of one ever again.

And this is not the worst that you will see. Even where teachers are the kindest people in the elementary school world, even when students love them, and gather around their desks to be near them, to joke and laugh with them, to bask in their affection and praise, you will see how these little people, so proud and eager and brave and curious in small groups with others like themselves, are reduced to shaking, anxious, tearful little shadows of themselves when they are required to do what most children dread, and are not prepared at all to do: stand up, alone, in front of their peers, and deliver a speech, or a book report, with thirty pairs of eyes all focused on them, thirty minds all prepared to consider them as foolish as the owners of those eyes dread being.

You will see that one teacher in ten thousand will empathize with these children, or will prepare them emotionally for this experience. And you will want to leap out of your seat and hug them all, and kneel down on the floor with them packed tight around you, and tell them, "It's all right, it's all right, it's all right. It's not your fault, it's not your fault, it's not your fault. There are other ways to show what you understand, better ways, wonderful ways, with no fear at all, no fear."

I was not warned, did not realize how it would be, had to sit still and listen, that first day, and watch even the proudest stumble through their handful of memorized lines:

Thomas Jefferson was born here, and studied there, and went there, and Alexander Hamilton did this, and did that, and Arizona is a nice place to visit, and the Grand Canyon is there, and its capital, Phoenix, is there, and it is bordered by, and if I were a passenger on a slave ship, I would, and if I were abandoned on an unknown planet, I would.

Their teachers said, "Okay, good. Okay, good. Okay, good," but it was not good, and all those humiliations and all those feelings of defeat and hopelessness and misery piled up and up and up, with every speech, and every book report that any child ever gave.

The best I could do immediately after one of these sessions was to print out thirty copies of one of my "papers," with this question on it: "How do you feel when you are required to give speeches and oral book reports?"

How did they feel? They felt like this: I think I am in front of a firing squad, I feel like I am going to die, I wish I was in California, I feel like a prisoner, I wish I didn't have to do it, I think I'm going to be laughed at if I say something wrong, I feel like 1,000,000,000,000 people are watching me, I feel like an idiot on stage, I think I am going to drop dead, I feel like I am going to get a U Minus, I think I am about to scream, I feel like I am tongue-tied, I think mine will be the worst, I think I am going to faint, I feel like running away, I think my pants are going to fall down, I feel silly, I feel like running down the hall into the bathroom, I wish I didn't have to go to school, I feel like crying and running away, I feel like I don't have any good books, I feel like I'm going to have a heart attack, I feel like a dumbbell, I feel like I'm going to throw up, I feel like the people are Martians staring at me, I feel like a nut, I think I am stupid, I feel like a dunce, I think I am going to get shot, I feel like Raymond sat on me.

YOU DON'T HAVE TO BE ALONE

"It's hard to stand up here, when you're small," I said, "when you're not used to it. Many of my college students aren't comfortable with it either. But I know of a good way to help you feel more comfortable up here, and I'd like to teach it to you."

One of the scariest things, for a lot of people of all ages, I told them, is feeling as if they are all alone, and are the center of attention. Another is feeling that they have to perform well, maybe even perfectly, or something terrible will happen. When you're scared like that, I said, it's very hard to remember what you want to say.

The best thing I knew, I went on, was to give each speaker some "helpers." In our experiment, we would need two speakers at a time, and a helper for each speaker, plus two other helpers who would write on the board behind them. It would be great, I told them, if each person could have the chance to be a helper, because helpers really did *help*.

Helpers A and B would stand next to speakers A and B and give them ideas in case they forgot what they were going to say. Helpers X and Y would write on the board what the speakers were thinking and feeling, even if it didn't show. For example, the speaker might say, "I think you're full of baloney," when, really, the speaker might be feeling, "Boy, it's scary up here."

Now, with helpers in place, I asked students to volunteer to role-play one of several situations I had written on cards. The first was this: "Sandy has been playing baseball in the street, and has just hit the ball through his own living room window. What happens next?" Sandy said, incredulously, that this *very thing* had recently happened at his house, and he would like to be in the skit. I asked him to play the role of his father, which he eagerly agreed to do. Marianne volunteered to take Sandy's role. We arranged the speakers and helpers. The front of the room, which had felt so open and so vulnerable before, now had me in it, plus six children, each with a specific task.

"Okay," I told the class. "Now, this is not easy, as you know. Sandy and Marianne need quiet so they can put themselves into the situation and really try to imagine how it might feel."

The room was instantly absolutely quiet. I suggested that Sandy and Marianne close their eyes for a few seconds, breathe, relax a minute, let the scene fill their minds.

Sandy, as his father, began.

Father *(loudly, angrily)*: All right! Who did this? Whoever did it will get a spanking. How many times do I have to tell you not to play base-ball in the street? Do what you're told, and this kind of thing won't happen. I'll take the money out of your allowance until this window is paid for!

Son *(scared, almost in a whisper)*: But I didn't do it on purpose. It was an accident!

Father *(still loud and angry)*: I don't care whether it was an accident or not. It was careless and stupid of you. Get in the house and go to your room!

Son *(still in a whisper)*: Okay.

The class, which had been thoroughly engaged, applauded.

I asked the helpers if they would like to add anything.

"My father would have *beat* me," one helper said.

"But he *really* didn't do it on purpose," said the other. "So it's not right to punish him too much. Everybody is careless sometimes."

Sandy told us what actually happened at his house and volunteered that Marianne had done a very good job being *him*. The writers at the board had written, for the father, "Angry, irritated." For the child, they had written, "Scared." One suggested that if the son had broken *some-body else's* window, the father might be *worried* too.

I asked if anyone in the audience would like to share experiences re-lated to the skit. Many hands went up, and boys and girls alike told how frightened they had been when they had broken something. I asked them to spend the last part of the class period writing me "a little note" about one of those times. They didn't have to sign their names if they didn't want to.

On several occasions, we did role-playing like this, until everyone who wanted to participate had participated. Occasionally, the central figures didn't know what to say. They stopped, consulted their helpers for ideas, remarked something like "Oh, okay," and went on. As far as I could tell, they were not afraid, and they focused well on the subject of their role-playing, and on the particular task for which they had volunteered.

GRIM DAYS

There were days when the silence in Mrs. Marshall's room was so tense that no one dared to break it by speaking to me, when everyone bent close to a book, a workbook, or a composition and said nothing to anyone.

What had she said, or done, to achieve this? She had assigned one student per row as the student monitor for that row. If anyone in the row got up out of his or her seat to approach Mrs. Marshall's desk, if anyone so much as sharpened a pencil, or dropped a book, or looked out the window, or asked a classmate a question, the *row monitor* would have to miss recess.

In this way, Mrs. Marshall turned her students' anger toward each other. The row monitors began to sound like their teacher. "You know the answer to that question! You heard what she said about that! You know you're not supposed to be out of your seat! Sit *down*, or we'll all get in trouble!"

On such days, I did not sit down. I tiptoed around the room, read bulletin boards, stood looking out the window, and let them work. I understood that everyone there had reached, or exceeded, his or her capacity for misery. But the next day, after the class was over, I would ask for time during my following visit—fifteen minutes, twenty-five minutes, whatever Mrs. Marshall could spare.

I learned that one grim day would take many weeks to get over. During those weeks, there might be more grim days. Grim days have a cumulative effect on the psyches of eight-year-olds, just as they do on people of any other age. They become wary. They become resigned. They close themselves down. They shift into a survival mode, a mode that children or adults find exhausting and demoralizing.

Grim days made it clear to me why I was never able to get rid of the backlog of griefs that these students felt, even though I was there for ten years, even though I listened and empathized, and provided outlets and alternatives over and over and over.

After a grim day, students would fill every line on my "papers":
Sometimes I get so mad I could _____,
Sometimes I just feel _____, especially when
_____. Right now I feel
_____. I feel like _____. I wish
_____. Then I could _____. But
_____. School is like _____ because
_____.

Sometimes they got so mad they could bite their skin, they could throw a riot party, they could scream, they could scream louder, they could overboil, they could melt the snow, they could tear themselves apart, they could rip the school in half, or even in fourths, they could kill themselves, they could kill someone mean, they could kill everyone, they could tear everything apart, they could hit Mrs. Marshall, they could pick up their desks and throw them at her, they could flush her head down the toilet, or even shoot her, they could throw up, and get sick, they could cheat, they could beat up their brothers or sisters, they could pull someone's hair out, they could break someone's leg, they could roar like a lion, they could eat people and dogs, they could die and bury themselves, they could sink into the ground and melt, they could go to heaven, where they would be safe at last, where they would be surrounded by all that was good, and free of all meanness.

When school was out, they felt happy. When school was in session, they felt stupid and horrible and bored, they felt like crying, they felt sorry for themselves, they felt sunk, as if they had just lost the Super Bowl, they felt steaming hot, they felt pale, they felt weird, they felt rotten. They dreamed scary dreams. They dreamed that a vampire came and tried to bite them. They dreamed that they would have to go to the hospital. They dreamed that they could play all day. They wished there were no such thing as school. School was like a jail. School was like a graveyard, because it had killed kids. They wished someone would close it down.

JUST IMAGINE

It was our last day in third grade. Composition books had been turned in. Spelling tests were done. There were no more reading assignments and no more reading comprehension groups. Mrs. Marshall had nothing planned and was happy to spend that last period working at her desk. I was more than happy to have the period to "do something."

"I know you're all tired," I said. "I know you can hardly wait to start your vacation, but suppose we just relax and use this hour to give our imaginations time to shift gears. I have a few questions. All I ask is that you be fifty-one percent serious when you answer them. When we're done, I'll sit out in my car and read what you've said, and then I'll put these papers in a box under my bed, where the rest of our papers are."

"Boy!" said one student. "You must have a lot of papers under your bed!"

It's true. And they've overflowed into the attic, and the living room as well—packet after packet, marked "Ten-Year Project: Third Grade, Fourth Grade, Fifth Grade, Sixth, Seventh . . ."

This is what thirty eight-year-olds had to say on their last day of third grade.

Why does the snow want to get into the ground?
To dance.

Why aren't there gentleman bugs?
Because gentlemen don't bug people.
So the ladybugs won't get married.

Why are ships and hurricanes named after women?
Because women are more intelligent than men.
Because women are very important.
Because women are very strong.
Because women are so sas-a-frassy.
Because men like girls.

Why doesn't toothpaste taste like apple pie?
Have you ever tried to stick a big pie
into a little tube?

When do flowers sneeze?
When they catch the cold.
When the wind blows.
When bird feathers tickle them.

When they can't blow their noses.
When they are pulled from the ground.
When they see a bee.
When they see Mr. Johnson.

Why don't rivers flow upstream?
Because they can't stand the muscle tension.

If you mixed a food you like with a food you don't like, what would you get?
Food for the birds.
Asparapiz.
A medieoaker food.

If you could break something, what would you break?
Mr. Johnson's nose.
A million-dollar vase.
Peter's mouth.
School.
School.
School.
School.
School.
School.
School.
Miss Gill.

Where were you before you were born? What were you doing?
At the grocery store, buying a banana split.
In Africa.
At your house, playing a game.
Up at my aunt's, eating breakfast.
In Hawaii, surfing.
Watching football.
Playing baseball.

What is under the ice at the North Pole?
The last dinosaur.
Baby fish.
The secret of Jack's craziness.
A suitcase.
A monster.
Fish with goose bumps.

What is the most magical thing in the world?
When I got a star on my spelling test.
A trash can.
Disappearing. Because your mom
would think you were wonderful.
Brian's mouth, because it can't be stopped.
How the earth got here, because nobody nose.

What would happen if you and Miss Gill ran the school?
We would run the school away.
I would receive $999,999,999,999,999,999,999,
999,999,999,999,999,999,999,999,999,999,999. . .
and we would give everyone in school a penny.
No one would have homework. No one would have to
stay after school.
A miracle.
Things would go crazy.
Man teachers would teach boys and lady teachers
would teach girls.
We would have lots of fun and not have to do any work.
I would gag Alex and tie him up.
We would change all the rules, get rid of the princible, and
eat candy and chew gum any time you want to and have good
meals and get a lot more food on your plate.
I would tie her up and take over.
The kids would have candy gum ice cream every day.
We would make recess two hours.
I would let all the kids that don't want to come to school,
let them stay at home.
I would fill it up with dynamite and blow it up.
There wouldn't be any school.

CHAPTER 2

Very Like a Jail: Ten Years in Public School

VERY LIKE A JAIL

They have given me these small pieces of their lives, these daisies and daffodils, these fishing lines and these worms wiggling, these conversations on the steps near the office, these sunny days with their faces all smiling and laughing in the windows, and nobody else has them, nobody. I have them all—and they, themselves, have forgotten them, have put them somewhere, under *their* beds, perhaps, in houses they visit only on holidays. And, when they go there, their minds are not where they used to be, and may never be where they used to be again.

They may never remember how full of promise they were, when they were eight, and in third grade, with a teacher who resented their giftedness and who tried her hardest to show them that, really, they had no imagination and no creativity and no vocabulary that was worth anything, and no maturity and no work ethic and no drive and no knowledge and no good points at all, except for their high IQs.

I know they hoped, at first, that I could save them, that, together, we would pack our bags and head for a better universe that didn't include school as we knew it—a place of rules and work and rules and work and rules and work, with no fun in it, except during lunch and recess and library, a place where kids' minds and kids' wishes didn't count for anything, where they were just prodded to perform, and fill in blanks, and read readers, and answer questions that made even the teacher yawn as she asked them.

In elementary school, boys and girls alike wanted to become Jaws and eat the mean teachers. They said school was like a prison, because you had to go there, whether you wanted to or not, because those in charge didn't even respect your basic human dignity, much less love you and show affection for you, and because the constant work you did there consisted of unproductive, boring routine. On days when they had to give book reports, and on many other days, they wished they could stay home. When they had to be there, no matter how they felt about it, they wanted to burn the place down, get rid of it, go home, play baseball, ride bikes, do anything, as long as it wasn't homework, as long as it didn't have anything to do with school.

This didn't mean that they were sick, or hostile, or unpatriotic, or poorly adjusted. It meant that schools, as they knew them, weren't places where they were free to think, to have adventures, to create, to find meaning and pleasure in reading and writing, to work together at tasks that were worth accomplishing, to take time to relax and "just live," to be in the company of adults who loved children and who were themselves happily and meaningfully engaged. It meant that schools weren't places where kids could thrive. They understood this very well. And most of the time, they didn't know what to do about it, except resent it.

I had promised them that I would be there in fourth grade, and again I visited twice a week, sat in their midst, listened to their whispered conversations, passed their notes on, observed reading groups, read compositions, copied spelling words off the board, talked with them individually and in small groups in the back of the room, by the windows, on the floor, talked with their teachers, and took over the class just as regularly as before.

Their fourth grade teacher was kind, open, friendly, patient, supportive—everything Mrs. Marshall had not been, but on their "papers" for me, which they continued to ask for, they continued to fill in almost all the blanks with their anger, not anger at their current teacher, but at Mrs. Marshall and other "mean teachers," and, sometimes, at each other. In spite of the fact that they never had to spend a minute in Mrs. Marshall's presence this year, they were still filled to overflowing with resentment toward her.

In fifth grade, it was the same. Their teacher was not mean-spirited, did not require absolute stillness and silence, did not jerk them into face-forward positions, as Mrs. Marshall had done. She did not yell at them, call them names, tell them they had mediocre minds. The worst she did was tell them that they were not to regard themselves as children any longer; they were to think of themselves as small adults. She told them they were to use "big words" as often as possible, and were to try not to use little ordinary words, which were boring and inadequate. This alarmed *me*, but as far as I could tell, they just accepted it as "teacher talk" and went on as they had been going on. They were not unduly tense in her class, did not write, any longer, about wanting to burn the school down.

In sixth grade, which was part of middle school, more, of course, was expected, and the focus on fancy, impressive words continued. Reading assignments were more intellectually challenging. Many students, mostly boys, read *Lord of the Rings*, and, following my advice about including helpers at the front of the room, performed skit after skit based, sometimes quite loosely, on their reading. Their teacher had a sense of humor, did a great deal of reading herself, liked having bright children in her classes, and praised them often. Students from other elementary schools were now mixed in with those I had already spent three years with. "My kids," I observed, in a conversation with one of them, never swore in their papers for me; the new students swore all the time. I asked him why this was. "Oh," he said, "That's because you let us do that in third grade. It's *boring* now."

In sixth grade, the boys seemed quite content, free to clown around in class, as long as they didn't carry it to extremes, free to experiment with their approaches to book reports and compositions, free to move around the room, have conversations with the teacher as if she were "an ordinary person" and not always an authority figure. They knew she thought about *life*, and not just about school, and grades, and order in the classroom. She asked them to think about such subjects as the causes of war, and prejudice, and death—subjects their past teachers had not discussed. She asked them to think about the chances of war in the future.

Many of the girls, meanwhile, became very catty, and criticized each other unmercifully if they did not dress the way they dressed, or behave as they behaved. Many times, when I arrived in the morning, those who were teased and criticized the most were standing tearfully alone in the hallway, trying to gather the courage to go back and face their overbearing peers.

A large cluster of these same students were placed in a special enrichment class, which they thoroughly enjoyed. Their teacher was probably the most energetic and accepting teacher in the school. The class met in a nontraditional room around a long, wide table, seminar-style. Rows of seats were gone. Lock-step assignments were gone. Students were free to dream, to imagine, to try out ideas. Some borrowed a wind power book from me, and the next time I visited, they were trying to figure out a way to hook up a television in their tree house. Computers were just beginning to be popular, and a few students were instantly addicted to them, playing computer games for hours on end, doing their best to test the games' limits, and laughing uproariously when they thought they had outsmarted the game's designer.

It was a nice break for them, a break all the other students would have welcomed, and profited from too—a place with few rules, a place to relax and think for themselves, a place where the teacher was on their side, and a place where imagination reigned.

In seventh and eighth grades, there was no enrichment class, and teachers were grim again. Imagination was out. Playfulness was out. Humor was out. Silence and hard work were in. Term papers were in. Three-by-five note cards, and proper footnote form, and data, data, data were in. The children felt now, for sure, that their childhood was just about over, but they did not worry that they might be unintelligent. They knew they were bright and knew that they were expected to work hard. Unfortunately, what they also knew was that school was becoming boring and meaningless, that it was having less and less to do with what mattered to them, and more and more to do with following rules, producing answers that pleased teachers and that did not rock any boats. They felt as if they were standing on the shore now of a huge and wonderful ocean, in a place where no one built boats and had long ago forgotten what boats were. They were expected to turn their backs on the ocean, enter the nearest factory, shut the door, and become part of the established factory routine. They saw no alternative to this. The factory had no windows, no light, and no view. It was painful in the extreme, to turn away from all that was beautiful and exciting and important to them, but they all did it.

In ninth grade, they entered high school, a more sophisticated place, with more windows. Some of them opened. Most of them did not. From the outside, this place looked light and free. There was grass, and sky, as a character in Melville's "Bartleby the Scrivener" says in the end of that story.

In this new factory, students were to do what they were told, without questions and without thought. They were to mimic their teachers' opinions, flatter them, agree with their world views, answer yes and no questions with yes, perform as their teachers wished them to perform, and, above all, make their teachers look good.

Prior to this time, when I arrived to talk with them, all these students loved to write with me. They remembered my "papers" from elementary school and continued to talk about all the sorts of subjects they had talked about before. The drudgery of eighth grade turned them against writing. The total dishonesty that was required of them in ninth grade made them hate it. I had always asked them, "Would you like to talk or write today?" Until now, they had always requested that we do both. Now, they asked that we not write at all, ever. Writing had lost its pleasure, and its meaning. Teachers, they said, did not want what they really thought. Teachers did not want to know how they really felt. Teachers did not want what they cared about. What did they want? They wanted "fancy bullshit," as one student described it. They wanted what had nothing of themselves in it. When they took themselves out of their papers, their teachers gave them A's. They wanted A's. They were planning to go to college, after all. They had to think, now, about their grade point averages. They had to please their parents. Most of their parents did not realize that they had to choose against themselves in this way. Most of their parents expected high grades. Some demanded them, measured their children's progress and maturity entirely by grades.

One teacher was another Mrs. Marshall, a Mrs. Marshall with a vengeance, a cocky, know-it-all gatekeeper, with an ego problem, as the students said. I visited that class, watched, listened, saw how it was. Later I took an entire college class there to teach poetry one on one to a class of students who hated poetry. I saw how he was—a teacher who told demeaning "jokes" about students, who thought his own jokes were funny, who gave low grades to anyone who told a similar "joke" about *him*, a teacher who enjoyed having power over the brightest students, who enjoyed threatening them with low grades, bullying them, intimidating them.

Several teachers were fussy about exactly where to write one's name on a paper, and where to write the page numbers, and how wide the margins needed to be. These same teachers had lists of rules for classroom behavior. You may do this; you must not do that. These rules were established by the teacher, had not been changed for decades, and did not allow for any student input. The same teachers lectured, paced back and forth, wrote on the board, talked as if no persons were in the room at all, just, perhaps, tape recorders. They used their lecture as an excuse to digress, to talk about sports, to talk about their home lives, to go on, at length, about anything that occurred to them. Students were to "show respect." This meant that they were to sit in silent appreciation and not protest. Never, ever, was it appropriate for them to design their own learning tasks or to explore something that they believed had not been explored before. There was no exploring here, no sense of adventure, no way to be engaged. Exploration, adventure, and engagement were not valued at all, were totally inappropriate. "Maturity" and "good manners" meant putting these values aside and allowing teachers to enjoy delivering their monologues to their captive audiences.

And so now, in our small groups of students taken out of study hall, we talked. We talked about these things, we talked about college, about getting drivers' licenses, about underage drinking, about friendship, about dating, about sex, about problems at home, about living, about dying, about loneliness, about boredom, about discouragement, about embarrassment, about humiliation, about defeat, about victory, about happiness, about fun, about religious beliefs, about values, about what a meaningful life was, and might be. I attended almost all their football games, basketball games, concerts, and plays. We talked about them. We talked about anything else they wanted to talk about, and could bring themselves to talk about. We talked through ninth, tenth, eleventh, and twelfth grades. In their senior year, I also started weekly dialogues on Sunday night in my home for anyone who wanted to talk longer, or talk more privately.

In high school, there were only two teachers who earned these students' trust: their former Enrichment teacher, who had "moved up" to high school, and their drama teacher, who, in addition to her regular teaching load, also directed the annual high school musical. They loved these two teachers, trusted them, talked with them, did their best for them, felt known and appreciated by them.

In second grade, these students had been blessed with another teacher they loved, and had been free to imagine and create. They had made an airplane, complete with steering wheel and windshield, and a cockpit large enough for several students to sit together there. This creation sat in the back of the room in third grade, where it became a reading retreat. To my knowledge, it was the last imaginative, meaningful thing these students ever created in school.

These same students could read at high school levels in third and fourth grade. They loved reading when they were young. But graded readers, book reports, and the constant focus on format, on grades, and on the number of books read killed their interest in books.

These same students had large, interesting, useful vocabularies in third grade. They had more exciting stories to tell than anyone had time to hear. But compositions with required numbers of sentences and paragraphs, points off for every possible mechanical error, weekly spelling tests on words that students had no share in choosing, words that had no emotional meaning, and teachers who were not also writers, or even researchers, who valued going through motions, who lacked humility and grace, who did not love writing, who were not introspective, who did not place a high value on empathy or on integrity, killed their interest in writing.

They graduated with honors, with high honors, with highest honors. Almost all of them went on to four-year colleges, and graduated from college. But their spirits were abandoned at the end of second grade, and, in the ten years I visited them, it was only too clear to me that their schools were filled mostly with busy work and with empty, mind-numbing routine. Any meaning they found they found outside of school, in their private emotional lives, in their friendships, and, sometimes, in their families.

What did it mean, then, to be labeled "gifted"? What did it mean to have high IQs, to be considered by their teachers to be the brightest students in their grade? Little that was good, wonderful, exhilarating, valuable, or even useful. And it meant a terrible waste of time, energy, and imagination, an immeasurable loss of joy in discovering and creating, joy in being what one was, and in what one could become.

This does not mean, of course, that school ruined these students' lives. It means that, when they saw and understood how limited their schools were, they withdrew their spirits, and kept their spirits to themselves, where they were safe. It means that they postponed their living, that they "lived" outside of school, after school. It means that they gradually "forgot" about school, about what it did for them, and what it didn't do. It means that they are shaping their own lives as well as they can. And it means that they will send their children to schools that will be as meaningless as those they attended, unless something very large is done to change them, to make them places where children can thrive.

"HEY! MISS GILL!"

> "I'd take a look at my own self in the mirror and wonder how it was possible that anybody could manage such an enormous thing as being what he was."

Chief Bromden, in Ken Kesey, *One Flew Over the Cuckoo's Nest*

"Hey! Miss Gill!"

"What!?"

"I can't write this letter!"

"Because you didn't like the visitor's presentation?"

"Yeah."

"Hm-m-m. Well, it's true that she took time out from her work to come and talk to the class. She would probably be glad to be thanked for that. So maybe you could say something about that, and then add, *But . . .* and say something, politely, that you would really like her to think about."

"Yeah! Okay!"

Dear Mrs. X. Thank you for coming to talk to our class. Maybe you could come back another time and listen to what we *have to say.*

*

"Hey! Miss Gill!"

"What!?"

"I just wanted to tell you that you have a great set of teeth!"

"Oh! Thanks!"

*

"Hey! Miss Gill! Did you see what I gave Mrs. Marshall for Christmas?"

"Yeah! I did!"

He gave her a large, stuffed shark, with a huge, wide mouth, full of teeth. It floated on Mrs. Marshall's desk now, its mouth pointed directly at her.

*

"Hey! Miss Gill!"

"What!?"

"Read my third one. I think I'm getting too goofy!"

"What's A. C.?"

"That's before B. C. I think I went too far back!"

"I think I know what you mean. You're saying that, before there were people on the earth, and even before there were dinosaurs, there were Greek sculptures! So they're really old!"

"Yeah!"

*

"Hey! Miss Gill!"

"What!?"

"Want to read my story? It has three installments! It might have *ten* before I'm done with it! It's about Mary and Art and me searching for the ghost rider. We end up in a castle. We walk really close together, because we're scared. We're almost scared enough to go back home!"

"I bet! Who's Mary, in the story?"

"That's *me*! Come and read *my* story!"

*

"Hey! Miss Gill!"

"What!?"

"Here's a picture of a horse's stomach!"

"Pretty gross, huh?"

*

"That's neat, the way you're drawing the branches. Do you think animals are hard to draw?"

"No, because I used to live on a farm in the midwest, and there were cows and things all the time. We used to go into a storm cellar when we heard the whistle. That meant *tornado warning*. They had police patrolling the roads. When we came out, there were fallen trees everywhere."

"You remember a lot, considering that you were not even four years old at that time!"

"How can you forget a tornado?!"

"Good point!"

*

"Have you heard of Clifford?"

"No, I haven't. Who's he?"

"He's a giant dog. Can I read you the story?"

"Sure!"

"What's that book you guys are reading?"

"It's about the dog named Clifford."

"Sounds like a good one."

*

"I've decided your name is *Polish*!"

"*Gill* is *Polish*?!"

"Yeah!"

"What do you know about that!"

"Dave's name means *nerd*!"

"Huh! My name is over seven hundred years old, and it means *Great Ruler*!"

*

"I'm taking the wheels off this model car and making a cannon out of it to shoot you with."

"I'll protect myself with my tablet!"

"That's not enough!"

"Then I'll protect myself with this snow-covered mountain on my notebook!"

"That's not enough either! Hey! You know what? I brought my microscope to school today! Want to see it?"

"Boy! That's exciting!"

"It took me a long time to get it ready!"

"I bet it did!"

POEMS

The fifth grade teacher handed out pages and pages of "fancy synonyms" of common words, intending thereby, as the directions on
some of them explained, to improve her students' vocabularies. Don't
use words like "big, small, old, young, happy, sad, beautiful, sour,
cold, red, green, blue, hot, rich, fat, or thin," suggested one sheet.
These are not interesting words. Look in a dictionary or a thesaurus for
more interesting words and refer to them when you write. To express
or describe love, affection, concern, try admired, altruistic, adorable,
charitable, cooperative, optimistic, reasonable, receptive. . . . To describe joy, try amused, blissful, ecstatic, magnificent, triumphant, vi-
vacious. . . . To express depression, try abandoned, battered, despised,
downtrodden, forsaken, estranged, discarded, downcast, obsolete, os-
tracized, regretful. . . .

Then came "poetry"—a word that chills the bones of most children
because it is presented in that same "Let's all try to impress everybody
as often as we can" way. Poems, to most public school teachers I
know, must rhyme, must scan, must follow this rule and that, must
seem, rather than *be*, poems, must not let a real feeling or a real insight
slip through, must not startle, must not move, must not touch, must not
be anything except one more clever, not to mention impressive, performance.

On Tuesday, Wednesday, and Thursday, the teacher handed out her
lists of synonyms, her rules for poetry and paragraphs. On Friday, I
gave them my page:

Some Theories To Try Out
What is a poem? Where does a poem come from?
1. One famous person said poems have to rhyme. Another person said
   they don't have to.
2. One famous person said poems should sound like fancy talk. Another said they should sound like ordinary talk.
3. One person said poems are quiet. Another said poems are loud.
4. One person said poems are happy. Another said poems are sad.

5. One person said poems start with "a lump in the throat" (Thompson 1970, 65). That same person also said that they start with "delight" and end with "wisdom" (Frost 1949, viii).

6. One person said a poet knows exactly where his poem will end. Another said a poem is a surprise to himself. He doesn't know what he's going to say. He says one thing, which makes him think of the next thing, which makes him think of the next thing, etc.—until he feels "done."

7. One person said poems are for everybody—all places, all times, all ages. Another said poems are something special between the writer and the reader, and a lot of other people just wouldn't understand, and didn't want to understand.

8. One person said a poem is "like a piece of ice on a hot stove." Once it gets started, it swirls around and around until it "melts" (Frost 1949, v).

Let's experiment.

When I told them Robert Frost wrote that a poem began "with a lump in the throat," one student raised his hand and said he had a lump in his throat at that very moment, and he didn't know how to get it out.

I answered that sometimes you just need to sit quietly for a few minutes and let the lump in your throat speak for itself and write its own poem, and he wrote a poem called "Top Coat Flushing," which was about how his stepfather had beaten him with a heavy, wet, man's overcoat, and how, in the poem, he had managed to flush this overcoat down the toilet.

The next day, I brought this little boy an African violet, and told him that hitting someone with an overcoat was like hitting a flower with an overcoat, and it was good that the poem had flushed it away. I told him the flower would grow strong and beautiful, even though it was also fragile, if he could keep overcoats away from it, and give it a little light, and a little water, and a little warmth regularly. I suppose I should have told him to consult his thesaurus for a more sophisticated word than "flush," and I should have said, I'm sure, that "toilet" does not belong in any poem. I should have told him that no overcoat I had seen would fit in any toilet I had seen. But I did not.

WHEN LIFE IS NOT FUN

The fifth grade teacher required everyone to make a collage entitled "Life Is Fun" and then write a commercial to accompany it in which they attempted to "Sell Life." She did this because, she said, the students were going to be in middle school the next year and she was sorry to hear that so many middle school students got into drugs and, therefore, would never see another birthday or another Christmas.

I didn't point out to her that students who abused drugs and alcohol obviously were not experiencing life as "fun," and that, when life was not fun, a little speech about how much fun life was would go over about as well as an announcement that the school district was moving to a twelve-month schedule. I asked for a chance to take over the class and drafted the following fill-in-the-blank exercise, which students could use, or not use, as they wished, to write a letter to themselves, which I would save, and, when they were adults, mail to them.

The blanks said this: When I'm really unhappy, scared, angry, worried, hurt, disappointed, bored, when life is not fun, I hope I will _____. I will tell myself _____. I will try not to _____. I will try to _____.

It would help to remember that _____. It would help me if I thought _____. It would help me if I knew _____. It would help to talk to _____. It would help if _____ told me _____ or just _____.

Every student responded to this exercise, and almost all of them used my format. Several said that, if life was not fun, they hoped they would feel better soon, but if they didn't feel better, they would try to "beat up on the jerk who made their life bad." Some said that they would try not to think, because thinking would be painful. One said he would want to die. Most said it would be better if they could just express how angry they felt.

Some were reminded of past anger. One student said he would just go in his room and slam the door. Another wrote, "I punched my sister once, and I threw her on the floor." "When I'm unhappy anyone near me gets clobbered, killed, and beaten up," another said. And that was true, also, if he was angry, or if he was worried, or hurt. Another was afraid he *might* really hurt someone when he was angry, because it was hard to stop himself from punching someone. Another said that when she was angry, she tried to be by herself, so she could remind herself that life isn't always fun and that you have to be sad sometimes. It helped some to talk to somebody, or just to go outside and play, or ride a bicycle, or listen to the radio, or eat junk food.

One girl said she used sad times to reflect on a "super dream" she had. She told herself that some days were better than others, and that there would always be tomorrow. It would help her if she thought there *was* a tomorrow, and if she knew something about the problems other people had, so that she would not feel that she was the only one with problems. It would help her if she could talk to people who understood her.

Another said he would try not to cry. He would try to laugh. Sometimes he would tell himself that "Polacks aren't smart," but it would help him most if he could think that they *were* smart. It would help if he could talk to another Polack, and if that person could tell him that Polacks were smart.

One girl said teachers could help by giving children something to look forward to, like a special class trip or a class activity that was fun.

Another described how she was frightened to be left home alone, especially at night. She was frightened if the phone rang, or if she heard dogs barking. As soon as someone came home, she felt better.

One wrote: "Ive Eye Weore Weyse, Eye Wood Knot Wright Sow Batd, And Eye Wood Knot Spelle Sow Batd. Ime a rotton spallear. Eye wichs Eye cold Bee Batter Butd Itz thea Whey Eye doo. Signed: Some Body Spesial."

THE HORRIBLE CURICKLEEUM WORM

"In the Middle School on May 22, 1979, in Room 102," said Shahn, "Curickleeums were formed. Ever since that time they spread all over the world, and people all over the world were eating, killing, squishing, and smashing them all over the place. After a while all were killed except 1. But this one was Tall, Green, and Gruesom. I knew we had to meet. For days later we met. Me and It standing There. I made the first move. I bit his arm! It was howling in pain. I knew it was all over."

He said that Curickleeums are "a menace to society." They not only strangle people but they crawl up their legs and bite them. "And they tear up Pizza Parlors and Baseball fields. P.S.," he added. "There is a Curickleeum on your back!"

His friend Alex said there was "a hole town" of them named Curick-ulumville, where 444,444,499 Curickleeums lived, and all of them were "green, slimey, goochy, and groosom when they were born," and they got worse as they grew older, because, while they ate good things, like pizza and stromboli, they also ate "green beens, peppers and purple and green moldy mush and dirty toenails and fingernails." According to Alex, they were all alike, except for the color of their belly button, which might be "blue, green, red, yellow, purple, orange, brown, black, white, or any color inbetween."

A lot of them used to hang out around the pencil sharpener, because they washed their hair with "lignified pencil shavings." Their hair was always "braided in four different directions." When you looked over your shoulder, there were always more of them than you could count—following you, ready to attack.

TRUST

I heard a colleague say once that it didn't matter to him whether a student told the truth in his compositions as long as he had a good thesis sentence. At first, I thought he was joking, but he assured me that he was not.

I thought maybe he meant that honesty was messy business—too much emotion in it, too much that you couldn't predict or control. I thought maybe he meant that honesty on the part of the writer asked too much of the reader, that it took writing out of the realm of performance and put it in the realm of dialogue, which demanded that the reader come out of hiding as well. This would be a frightening possibility to someone accustomed to viewing writing as a spectator sport.

I've always felt it was a privilege to be trusted with something that cost something to say, with something that went beyond performance, that went beyond grades, that marked a realization, a struggle, a search, a resolution, that mattered for its own sake.

As I followed the gifted class into middle school, I thought of these things. I didn't know how to say what I was beginning to understand about the way schools were. It wasn't just a particular English teacher who didn't distinguish between honesty and dishonesty. There was something at least as large as the institution of school itself, and probably larger than that, that seemed distinctly Machiavellian, that seemed not to value integrity, and, that, therefore, did not, and could not, model it, so it settled for going through motions, and expected others to go through motions too. It paid lip service to authenticity, but, actually, it did everything it could to weaken and destroy it.

But if this were true, I realized, I didn't know *why* it was true. I didn't even know if there was a name for this deep and thorough lack of honesty, and lack of courage, and lack of faith that whatever was deeper than dishonesty would ever be accepted and, therefore, safe.

In my teaching, anywhere, it seemed to me, I was responsible for creating conditions where introspection and honesty could feel safe, and, to the degree that I myself could be transparent and trustworthy, others were likely to be transparent and trustworthy as well.

In college, I saw, almost everything students did was regarded by them, and by most of their professors, as a performance—usually, a performance for a grade. Professors, too, performed, were considered boring and old-fashioned if they didn't become entertainers in the classroom. All around me, it seemed, there was a kind of trade-off: I perform; you perform. You flatter me; I flatter you. It seemed as if this charade went on, year after year, and was rewarded.

The only alternative I saw was to reject the performance model altogether. In my college teaching, and in my work with the gifted class, I did my best to create a genuinely dialogical teaching model, where being was valued more than seeming.

All the way through the ten-year project, "mean, boring, and unfair teachers" dominated our discussions. But beginning in middle school, students' loneliness was a constant concern as well. Many students felt misunderstood, unappreciated, and unloved, and it made them wonder if anyone would ever take the time and make the effort not just to care about them, but to give them some sign that they cared, especially at the times when they felt most alone. It wasn't enough for parents and teachers to *tell* them that they cared. It wasn't a matter of *proving* that they cared. It had nothing to do with buying them expensive presents or taking them on trips. It was a matter of giving them a *sign*.

Each child knew what sign he or she wanted. It was always the same: "Take the time to give me your undivided attention. Take the time to listen to me without judging me, without making fun of me, without focusing so thoroughly on what you think I do wrong. Do this regularly, not out of habit, not out of duty, but freely, because you *want to*, and because you want me to feel safe and loved. And deserve my trust. Live the truth. Speak truthful words to me. Make your words count. Keep your promises. Admit it when you don't know something, or when you've been less than honest, or when you've made a mistake. Try to do better. Try to notice when you, yourself, fail to meet your own standards. Apologize. Set an example."

As the following seventh graders' remarks make clear, it is a rare adult who deserves a child's trust.

"I like it when people tell the truth, but not many people I know do," began one student. "When a person tells me a lie, I feel hurt, and wonder why they couldn't tell me the truth," another said. "When I'm telling the lie, I start to feel guilty and disappointed in myself. I know that after I tell the lie whoever I tell it to will get mad and probably won't be able to trust me any more. So I don't tell that many lies. When I'm telling the truth, I feel good about myself. I know I've done something good, that some people can't do. When I want to say the truth but I know it will hurt someone, I keep it bottled up inside me with the top on tight, and I just stay quiet and try to think of something I can say that would make them feel good about themselves, and me too."

Another said that her mother told her to lie when she answered the telephone, to say that she was not at home when she was. When she answered the telephone, she said, she stuttered.

One boy said he hated it when one of his friends lied to him. Once a friend of his promised to wait for him in front of his house while he ate supper. When he came back out, his friend wasn't there, and wasn't at his own home either. The next day, when he saw him, he asked why he had behaved that way. His friend's reply was "Just a little joke. Funny, wasn't it?" He didn't think so. He signed his writing exercise for the day "Friend of a Little White Liar."

"I feel very ugly at the moment, and I wish sometimes that I were dead," wrote one. "Today I feel rotten," wrote another. "In my family I feel left out. Nobody cares about me. My mom and my dad care about my brother and sister more than anything in the world, not about me. My mom says she cares, but she doesn't. Nor my dad."

"I don't think Mr. James likes me," confided one boy. "I don't like myself very much. I am frustrated with my life because it seems like life is just passing me by. I wish that I had something to look forward to."

"Someday I wish that my parents would realize that I'm a normal person, not gifted," a girl added. "I wish that they would realize that I need help with things. Sometimes I wish that I could learn to like myself as I am and not try to please everybody else. I wish I could just go home and do things that I want, not what everybody else wants. I wish I had a boyfriend. I wish that I was pretty and popular. And, finally, I wish that my parents would show that they love me."

Others said they hoped other countries would be friendly toward the United States. One hoped that no one would attack us with a nuclear bomb or start World War III.

Some played with the truth, even with serious truths, and wrote lies in order to convey the opposite of what their words said: "I never told a lie. I never got in trouble. I never struck out in a baseball game. I would agree with the umpire who said $4 + 4 = 20$. I never was mad at anyone. I never was very mad at someone. I cannot stand all sports. I think our team is rotten, stupid, dumb, ridiculous, scummy, terrible, and a stinky football team. I never met a person I did like. I never met a person I didn't like. I like any and everything. All lies are great. I never got in trouble for a lie."

"I love world geography. I like my brother. I'm pretty. I'm sexy. My parents love me. I like living at home and I want to stay there. I want to live. A lot of boys like me. I like to do things by myself. I like school."

One boy found this approach especially liberating, borrowed the title of one of my exercises, and discussed all his teachers, one after another: "Teachers lies, lies and more lies. Mrs. S. is considerate, skinny, helpful, courteous, beautiful, trustworthy, doesn't drive you to the looney farm, smart, organized, kind, nice, never yells, tells good jokes, doesn't give you too much work, runs a very nice class, very fair."

"Mr. T. lies, lies, and more lies. Has good taste in clothes, never talks too much, never plays with his sock, never wears pink, never sits cross-legged, always makes his class interesting."

"Mrs. V. lies, lies, and more lies. Never tells people to turn around when they're looking straight ahead, never has trouble moving around, never gives homework."

"Mrs. W. lies, lies, and more lies. Never has trouble controlling a class, never yells, never makes the students laugh at how stupid she is, never holds you after class."

"Mrs. Z. Always fair, never gives you insipidly boring work, never gets mad at the people who aren't doing her never insipidly boring work because they're too interested in it, never yells, shouts, screams, bellows, talks loudly, or gets mad."

THIS CLASS IS SO BORING!

When I visited high school classes, which I was invited to do only occasionally, I was struck, almost always, by what I would call the huge "human distance" between the teachers and the students. It was as if the teachers had done their best to separate their role as teacher from the "whole person" that they were and that they had been all their lives. And they had succeeded. They came with information, but it was all textbook information, which they themselves had studied somewhere, sometime. It was data in a vacuum. As "whole persons," they were simply not accessible to their students, and, perhaps, did not want to be.

They had taken on the role of authority and disciplinarian, but it was not what students could determine to be *earned* authority. It was not the authority that comes from integrating information into one's character and life, or even from reflecting on the possible uses students might make of it. It was not *trustworthy* authority. It seemed to be secondary to the teacher's role as disciplinarian, a role based solely on the fact that teachers were older and, usually, larger than the students, and, it was to be assumed, had the even greater disciplinary power of the school administration to back them up.

The gifted students, who were now in ninth grade, sensed the hollowness of this and had many opportunities to understand, more than they wished, how close this came to bullying.

It was clear to them that teachers had all the power, and students had next to none. Teachers could humiliate them in front of their peers, and could fail them, or prevent them from being on the honor roll, or prevent them from being accepted by the colleges of their choice. Teachers could make fun of students, but, beyond a minimal point, which was never quite clear to them, students could be reprimanded or punished for making fun of the teachers.

From third grade through ninth grade, I had already given them countless opportunities to talk out and write out their resentment of unfair and boring teachers, but, at times, it seemed to me that their supply of resentment was no less than it had been in Mrs. Marshall's class in third grade.

Why this was, I'm not entirely sure, but it seemed to me then, and it seems to me now, that all through school too many teachers routinely attacked the *character* of these students, routinely shamed them, in front of their peers, to demonstrate to them, and to the other students, how much raw power they had in the classroom. Many times, students felt required to take intellectual positions that they did not agree with in order to receive the grades they wanted, and they never felt it was safe to say this in the presence of their teachers. The teachers themselves, especially those in high school, seemed to enjoy knowing that they frightened and intimidated students.

The same teachers were criticized, year after year, for the same behavior. Nothing, it seems, was ever done about it. Neither parents nor students ever got together to plan strategy and meet with the teacher or the principal. This told me that no one expected these problems to be solved, and, therefore, there was nothing to do but to let off steam. Teachers could complain about students, and students could complain about teachers until those teachers retired and new ones, just as boring or unfair, took their places. Nothing would change. "Life is like that," some might say. "You have to choose your battles."

It's true, of course. You *do*. It's a pity, though, that no one chose this one. It might have been won. There would have been only one way to find out.

I listened to an entire year's worth of stories about the ninth grade teachers and asked students to imagine that they were writing a letter to the teacher who had contributed the most pain to their lives that year.

Many of my college students told me, routinely, how bored they were in their classes. What they meant was that they could see no use for the material that was being presented, most often by lecture, and there was no sense of connection between themselves and their professors. It meant that their professors did too much of the talking, and that their talk was almost exclusively monological. It meant that they did not feel free to speak about this, or to leave, because they needed the course to fill a requirement.

It is true that some teachers might be in the wrong profession, or might be burnt out, or might be preoccupied with difficulties in their personal lives, so that they have too little energy and time to think about what they might do differently, or too little courage or insight to try talking, and listening, in a different way.

It takes energy, courage, and insight to stop what one is doing, to admit to oneself that it is not working well, or that it is not working at all. It takes much more to put defensiveness aside and to discuss this frankly with one's students. It might seem to be almost a lapse in teaching etiquette to speak about the process of teaching and learning with students. It might seem like an admission that one is a failure, might result in diminished authority or respect, might, also, destroy some treasured illusions on both sides of the teaching/learning gap.

It must be painful to know that you have failed to make a meaningful connection, and to remain silent, to watch, daily, from your side of the gulf, and see the students, whose trust you want, and need, making fun of you, writing notes back and forth, totally indifferent to what you are there to do. So often, when teachers begin to realize how large the gulf is between them and their students, they do exactly the wrong thing: they go on talking when they should listen, they remain silent, or, worst of all, they lecture the students about the inappropriateness of *their* behavior, without accepting any responsibility for the classroom climate at all. They fill the empty spaces with noise, with static, to try to block out their own pain at having missed the chance to make a real connection with their students. Students' pranks and indifference, and perhaps even their anger, might be forms of blocking too. Perhaps whoever realizes that something needs to change bears the most responsibility for calling attention to that need and for taking at least some steps to open a dialogue.

In this case, the students felt that the teachers they criticized were indifferent to their needs, or, possibly, unable to meet them. They were not prepared to initiate any change.

They said, first, that one teacher spent most of their time together talking about the need for respect and the rest of the time criticizing students. When this teacher spoke, he paced back and forth and did not speak clearly. He was easily side-tracked, and enjoyed talking about football instead of the subject he was assigned to teach. In some cases, he went over material for a test too many times, and, in others, he did not go over the material enough. He had too many rules and paid too much attention to the format in which students were to take notes.

These were excellent criticisms, once their anger was siphoned off. There was nothing catastrophic about them. A teacher who can laugh at his or her own excesses, a teacher who wants to reach students, who has not given up on the possibility of reaching students, could easily consider them. But, for those who have long been out of touch with students, even the smallest change is threatening. Some might have built an entire career on just such professional distance, might never have experienced a real sense of dialogue, or closeness, or acceptance in the classroom. It is good for students to think about such possibilities and to consider how difficult change might be.

Their criticisms of another teacher also involved a number of complex issues, all of them important, and potentially helpful, as well. They said she seemed unable to hold the attention of ninth graders, and behaved as if she were used to teaching much younger children. She spoke to them as if they were in elementary school. Although she liked it herself, she had no idea how to present the course reading material in a way that would engage the students.

She could not establish any bond with the students at all, and she could not laugh at herself. She was so engrossed in the subject she was lecturing about that she was oblivious to the constant pranks that students played to entertain themselves during her class. They made bets with their classmates that they could inch their chairs from the side by the window to the side by the door, in one class period, without her realizing. They tied a rope to a radio, turned it on, and lowered it out their second story window without her ever noticing. Some of the students thought she was oblivious because she was an alcoholic. The others just said that she was boring, and they were not learning anything from her.

It might very well be that this teacher would have been more comfortable with younger students. Or, perhaps she *was* an alcoholic. But suppose she were intellectually, emotionally, and academically qualified to teach high school. Then the problem becomes this: how does one talk with high school students in a way that engages them and earns their respect? What if she is required to teach a text that students cannot get interested in? How would the students deal with such a situation if they were the teacher of students like themselves?

There may be no easy answers to such questions, but, if they are not asked by *someone*, classes such as these will never change.

LONELINESS

I don't think we realize how lonely children and teenagers are, in school, or, if we do, I don't think we realize how important it is to help them understand their loneliness and deal with it.

Ostensibly, my conversation with Janet was about one of her classes, which she considered boring and irrelevant. She didn't find much value in the academic part of school, and was not on the "academic track"; she planned to go to secretarial school. On interest tests, which she had recently taken, she scored high in secretarial areas and in mathematics.

In middle school, she had been peppy, interested, and enthusiastic, had talked easily. In high school, now, she waited for me to ask questions and seemed preoccupied, listless, tired, and resentful. She saw school as an imposition. No classes held her interest at all.

She began, wistfully: "Think you could arrange to get me out of science? That's my worst class. I can't get interested in it. It's too boring for me. All he does is talk, and I have no interest in what he's teaching."

What subject had he been lecturing on today?

"Oh," she sighed, "He's talking about bugs right now—about DDT, and all kinds of junk. We're on chemicals now."

She had no use for information about DDT.

This surprised me, because I knew she lived on a farm.

"Don't you spray your crops?" I asked.

Yes. But that was her father's job, not hers. She had no idea what chemicals were in the spray her father used, and had never thought about it, even during science class.

I wondered if her father were as quiet and reserved as she was, imagined myself as a farmer, reading all the labels, trying to learn how to run an organic farm, saw myself, for a moment, raising free-range chickens with no chemicals at all.

I thought about her science teacher, about the conversations I had had with him and his wife outside of school. Probably, I thought, she would find it much easier to talk with his wife, who was more comfortable with dialogue than her husband was, who seemed to enjoy it.

"You know?" I said. "I think our learning depends a lot on who we consider our teachers to be. I learn a lot from my vet. I really enjoy learning from him, and I like him a lot, as a person."

"Yeah," she sighed. "Teachers go about it the wrong way. They went to school. I don't know how to say it. They teach it in a professional way, and it doesn't really get through to you, what they're talking about."

I asked if there were anything about school that she liked.

"It's all right," she said, and paused for a long time. "I don't really like school that much."

"Because—"

"Because I'm not with any of my friends."

I listened to the sadness and disappointment in her voice. I hadn't realized this, had assumed that all the students I talked to were in the same academic program, and had the same classes and the same teachers. She had one friend in science—and no friends in any of her other classes. It made a long day—and a long year.

Remembering that she had written her career notebook on secretarial work, I asked if she really would enjoy that. She thought she would. She had talked to relatives who were secretaries, and they seemed to like it. She wouldn't consider a job that required four years of college, but she could handle secretarial school. She wished she could just quit school and get a job, not bother with any classes where she just had to sit there taking notes every day, but she knew that to get a decent job, she needed a high school diploma, at least. If those who did the hiring didn't care about her degrees or lack of them, she said, she wouldn't care either.

I was struck by her sadness, her feeling of isolation and meaninglessness, the feeling that school stretched on and on, with no purpose in it whatsoever for her. After she left, I sat there in silence, wondering if it would help her to have her friends with her, wishing I could make that happen. I thought how wrong it was, to have a system that didn't help students to find meaning in academic subjects, that didn't prepare teachers and counselors to think about students' emotional needs and to address them. How terrible, I thought, for a talented young person such as Janet to spend tenth grade like that, with nothing better to look forward to in eleventh grade, or twelfth.

HAVE YOU DONE YOUR HOMEWORK?

Today, Janet is reading a book about vampires. It's not boring, she tells me. School is what's boring. We have been through this territory before. Science is boring. She has no use for it. It is boring when teachers drone on and on about whatever it is they have decided to talk about. They're like a television stuck in the "On" position.

Erica is here today too. She finds study hall boring. I laugh. I never had a study hall, don't know what it's like to be required to spend an hour or so in silent reading under those conditions. I think I would get ahead on my homework, so I wouldn't have so much to take home. In my youth, I filled my study hall hours with choir and orchestra. I spent long hours, every night, with my homework spread out on my bed, or on the kitchen table, and worked until I finished it. If I had a lot, I did it on Friday night as well.

Erica volunteers that she is glad I took her out of study hall. I ask if she can relate to what Janet is saying, that her courses themselves are boring, that she doesn't know how to make them interesting for herself.

She says that math is like that, because, after the teacher explains what needs to be done, they "sit around and do homework" in class. If they finish early, they can talk if they're not too rowdy. Everyone finishes early, so every day they "sit around" in math class, waiting for the bell to ring. It's the sitting around that she finds boring. I'm surprised that class time is used so often for homework, even with the gifted class. I wonder how this counts as stimulation and enrichment—and why it never takes a full class period to teach math.

Janet and Erica tell me how their day goes. Every day begins with a reading, they say, then they all "rise and say the Pledge of Allegiance." They have four or five minutes of announcements, and then four or five free minutes. There are free minutes, but there is nothing to do in them. They wait them out—every day. "Free" means "free to waste." They haven't thought of bringing something interesting to school to do in that time. They wouldn't dream of asking the math teacher to work a little harder, give them harder problems, divide them into groups to solve them, send them outside of class to work on a math project, send them away from the clock, from the four-minute daily wasteland.

Parents must not realize that their children's days disappear in this way. You would think they would be at the door en masse, protesting not just about the waste of their tax dollars, but about the waste of their children's minds and lives.

I think how hard, and how long, these same children worked in third grade, writing book report after book report, turning in composition after composition, writing spelling words in sentences, copying this material or that off the board, drawing pictures, making notebooks, working every minute. I think about how much energy they had then, how rich their imaginations were, how much they enjoyed their minds. And it's come to this: "sitting around" in math class and study hall, with nothing that holds their interest, every day, waiting for the bell to ring.

IT JUST ABOUT PUTS YOU TO SLEEP

Jared tells me he thinks school has affected him a lot because he spends eight hours there every weekday. I ask him what, exactly, it affects. "My attitude," he says. I wonder what that means. It means that, on most days, he's so bored in school that he almost falls asleep, because there's nothing there to keep him occupied. In spite of that, his grades are in the high 80's, and would have been higher, except that he "messed up" on a couple classes.

So, I ask him, what does all that say about the way school affects him? He tells me that it says senior year in high school is pretty much a repeat of whatever he learned in his sophomore and junior years. School is supposed to prepare you for life. It's supposed to give you information that you might need someday. He doesn't think that's happened yet, and he's a senior.

Now it's time for him to think about getting a job—any kind of job would be all right, as long as it pays the minimum wage and gives him forty hours a week. Even a factory job would be okay. It doesn't matter. He just wants to earn some money.

It won't matter where he lives, really. He could live with his mom, or his dad, or his grandparents. "There's plenty of time to decide," he says. School won't be out for about seven months. He thinks he'll just "wait and see what comes around." A lot can happen in seven months.

I wonder what might happen in the next seven months that hasn't happened yet and ask if he ever considered going to college. Nobody ever suggested that, but it's crossed his mind. It's just that wanting to go and actually getting there are two different things. There's the money, first. But even if he had the money, he might not be able to "hack it." The worst part would be taking all those other classes, and not just the ones he was interested in.

He does have interests outside of school. He likes sports, especially basketball, because it involves teamwork. Everyone gets to do something to help score. Nobody's sitting around the way they are in class.

He's good at math, but math doesn't interest him at all.

I ask him if he feels he has a sense of purpose in his life. Nobody ever asked him that before. He knows some happy adults, he says, adults who just like what they're doing. "Every person has to be happy for something, right?" he asks me. "Probably my happiest time is when I'm sleeping."

His mom is happiest when she's talking on the phone to his sister, but she's pretty happy when he brings home his report cards. She thinks he's done pretty well, considering that required classes are so boring. Like English. "Because who's going to go around putting verbs in a sentence, or reading stories, and summarizing? The stories aren't about real life, and some of them are actually stupid."

I wonder which stories they are — the stupid ones, and think about talking without verbs. Actually, if we had to give up nouns or verbs, I'd rather give up nouns, make nouns into verb forms, get those heavy old nouns moving — wondering, being, talking. I think verbs could help Jared. I wish *I* could have helped him, could have plucked him out of high school at the first sign of uselessness and boredom and apprenticed him to a mad scientist, or a rock star, or an architect, or sent him to Habitat For Humanity, or — somewhere, where he felt interested, and useful, and appreciated, where he didn't have to sit still all day, and read stories that weren't about the real world — that is, about the world he woke up into, and went to sleep from.

THEY LIKE TO GIVE THEIR OWN THOUGHTS

They had a test on John Steinbeck's *The Moon Is Down.* The teacher changed it because some kids were giving out the answers. It was hard. They didn't know anything *about* Steinbeck. The question on the test was, "How is this novel a document of freedom?" They didn't know anything about it.

They got thirty-three points, just for reading it. Some people didn't even read it. They didn't read it because they are totally irritated with the teacher, because he won't give them a good grade unless they regurgitate. They don't want to regurgitate. They want to give their own thoughts. They're giving their own thoughts now.

"You don't learn," they say. "You don't learn."

Mr. Phillips is a pain in the butt. He likes the girls, but he doesn't like athletes. All the athletes got zeroes. They didn't read the story. He gave the same tests as last year. Brian got someone's notebook, and all the tests were in there. Everyone got a ninety. It was AB, ABA, BDA, AC, then blank, then BD, then blank, then BC. But he added another thirty points, and everyone bombed that part.

So what did they say about this "freedom" business? They told about how you can't capture a free man's mind. For extra credit, they had to read a quote from "Socrates' *Apology*" and tell what it meant.

They didn't even read the book. One read twelve pages. One read twenty-three pages. Another did that on *Tale of Two Cities* and got ninety-nine, on *Red Badge of Courage* and got ninety. They hardly read *any* of the stories. They don't *have* to, really. They don't even have to *listen* in class. They just sit there and pick on people. Because all they have to do is repeat what the teacher already got done saying. They can just tell by the way he's talking what he wants. The trouble is, if they say it was easy, then he gives them a zero for not trying. Jake told him it put him to sleep, so he gave him a zero too. They got a seventy if they had a run-on and a fragment, even if one of them was from the book.

He grades them for not liking him. One person got eighty for a marking period, his only C. It kept him off the honor roll and out of the honor society. That happened to somebody else too. It kept him off the honor roll too. One girl told him he should smile more. That got her a seventy-eight. She never got below eighty-five in English before, never got below ninety in her final average.

He's giving everybody a hard time. First test, the average must have been about fifty-six percent. He was telling everybody: "If you can't do it, you gotta get out now." Even if they work, they don't pass. This is their most important year, and he's "killin' 'em." Grammar wasn't so bad because "it's set." It wasn't "his personal thing." Now, when they're doing essays, and he doesn't like them, he can "hack them up." What he wants might not be what they think. If their ideas don't correspond with his ideas, they're going to get a bad grade. They talk about a story and figure out the most important elements and back it up with statements. If they think the setting is most important and back it up, and he thinks it is the plot, they'll be penalized. So they have to go with him—unless they're *dumb*. They have to remember what his tastes are and what he picks for questions.

One of his questions was: "What was the significance of 1808 to 1854?" They don't remember the exact dates. It was Poe's lifespan. "When we go off to college," one boy says, "do you think we're going to have to remember that date? How is that going to help us? We should know about his lifetime, but that's just trivial!"

One class member writes, "He could have his picture in the dictionary next to the word *hypocrite*. This man has the exterior of a person who truly believes he is the greatest gift to the world that could ever be given. He walks like someone who has his thoughts always on his own ego. He makes a living out of making jokes about people in the class that are not funny as far as *they* are concerned. He stifles their opinions by downgrading them and accepts only his own ideas. His mind is generally closed to outside observation. Reasoning with him is impossible. He uses a special kind of egomaniac logic. Any outbreak of anger at him spells the beginning of never-ending humiliation for the student."

So—what do you do with a teacher like that? What should the teacher do, if students don't read the assignment, and just guess, or get the answers from someone? Is that the only way for a free man to avoid having his mind captured? There is a wide, wide space for dialogue here.

LOVE IS TAKING TIME

She's seeing a psychiatrist because a couple months ago she tried to commit suicide. She tried it *twice*. It was because she had a low self-image, because she felt like a failure at eighteen, because all her friends were so pretty and talented. They were so popular and everything, and they always got elected to things, and she didn't, and she didn't have any talents. That really hurt her. So she wanted to kill herself, until Jason died, and then she realized that she didn't want to be dead and cold in the ground.

Her parents are going through a hard time. They might split up. Her father is a nice man, but she's not close with him like she is with her mother. He is very unemotional. He doesn't express his feelings, except he does have a very bad temper. She and her mother have a really good relationship. They always talk to one another about their troubles. Her mother is a fantastic lady. She works all the time, and she is still kind and giving and understanding. Her mother is always there for her. She is very supportive. Whenever she needs someone to talk to, she can count on her. She understands her feelings. She is always willing to help others, even if it takes up her spare time. She's very proud to have her as a mother. The only real chance they have to talk is while they do their hair in the morning.

Sometimes she feels really angry. She doesn't know why. She doesn't get angry very often, but when she does, she raises her voice and slams doors. That's when she goes out and rides her bike. She can never find anybody to ride with her, so she usually rides by herself. But she doesn't do that very often, because she's going to school, and she's holding down two jobs, and she doesn't have very much spare time really.

This is how love is, in the world we live in, which, as far as we know, is the only world there is. Love on the run. You've got to take as long as you can doing your hair.

"Being there" is sort of a figure of speech. "Let me know if you need me for anything," we say. "I'll try to fit you in, between the dentist and the oil change, between Safeway and the hairdresser's. We can talk while the kettle's boiling for tea, or maybe before I put the clothes in the dryer, or after I walk the dog. Let me check my calendar."

We put in an appearance or ten, convey our heartfelt sympathy while the motor's running. There's always somebody else who needs us, and somebody else after the somebody else. We could cross ten items off our list instead of two, two thousand instead of ten, if we could just schedule our time better. We could fit something in before the evening news, get a second job, go back to school, take in the Grand Canyon, go to Paris for lunch.

But somebody should say a little something about "talent" in this space, this flicker of incomprehensible light that has never been measured and never will be measured. "Pretty, and popular, and talented, and they always get elected to things." If you don't have all that, what *are* you?

Everything you were before, from your birth onward, and everything you will be, an ever-expanding universe on the *inside*, a miracle—unlike any other miracle anywhere, any time, eyes that see, eyes that can speak every language, ears that hear, a mind that works, a heart, feet that dance, hands that reach out, every small and large part as perfect and as beautiful as it's possible to be, impossible to improve upon, an *I* looking for a *thou* who understands these things, who knows what counts in the world.

How painful it is, to measure yourself by the wrong scale, to look in mirrors not your own. How terrifying it is, to think your mirror is too small when it is the only one you have.

Your talent is the song you sing when you are not on any stage, the good that you stretch yourself to reach, the silence afterward, the love you give yourself in this most present moment, even if no one else is there to understand or share it.

Don't ever underestimate your own vastness. And stand still, every day, long enough to know it's there.

MESSAGES

When Jason died, he left a message for the rest of us: he was an innocent victim of a stressful world, which, for some reason, he didn't feel a part of. He didn't know how to save himself. Others share the responsibility for his decision to end his life.

The message is that we need to listen and understand, and, somehow, we need to rejoice in our lives and in what they bring us.

If only we could find the faith we need to console us when we are afraid. If only we could go on expanding ourselves forever. If only we could feel that our lives are important enough to value.

*

It really upset me when I heard the news about Jason. I didn't know him very well. I had only one class with him that I remember. About one week before Christmas, we talked a little. I really don't understand why he would do it, but I know how upset I get when people put too much pressure on me. It still bothers me, and I still think about him a lot. I know that when I'm a parent, I will never push my children to live up to other people's standards. I will always try my best to understand my children's feelings and help them with their problems.

*

My parents are kind of disciplinary because most of the time I am around them, they are asking me to do something or telling me to do one thing or another. Both my parents are especially into discipline when it comes to schoolwork. Sometimes I wonder if I will ever have any time to myself. This is why I want to live in a dorm, then an apartment, when I go to college. I mean, I study hard, and I get good grades, but they are never satisfied. It's just been like that for as long as I can remember.

The teachers were like that, in grade school. They never gave us any real chances to prove our maturity. From grade one to the last day of grade five, it was the same thing day after day and year after year. Hardly anybody gave us any chance to do anything new and really grow. A few teachers tried it, and it went over well. I don't know why the rest of them didn't realize that you can't grow up if somebody is standing over you every minute and telling you exactly what they think you should do.

*

My father is very stubborn and set in his ways. Whatever he thinks of doing is right. When I do something that he doesn't like, he puts me down. He knocks all my friends (there's at least one thing wrong with all of them, so I shouldn't like them so much). Things he expects me to do that I don't do, he lets me know about. Then when I do do it, he doesn't say anything good about it. He just finds something that I did wrong. He doesn't appreciate my efforts. Since he didn't go to college, he doesn't think I should. One day, things were going bad, and I would cry at almost anything. We were talking about taxes and things, so I offered to help him, and he started in on the things I couldn't possibly know, like mortgage depreciation, so I started crying because he was near to yelling at me, and then he came in with, "How do you expect to be a college graduate when you cry when something doesn't go your way?" I just felt really useless and thought, "Well, why should I even try to do anything with my life?" These are times when I get real depressed and stressed.

*

After a while, you don't care about grades. You try to enjoy yourself. As you go through school, you say, "Heck with it. Enjoy it while you can, because the rest of your life you'll be working." So you do the things I do—date once in a while, party, play basketball, throw the javelin, go fishing, hang around with your friends, joke around, sleep. Work's important. Do the work, but try not to put as much into it. Try not to get as much stress. For me, I have to work. I'm not that smart. Some people are naturally smart. It'd be nice if I could be that way. I just try to do the best I can.

*

Teachers put too much pressure on you. They all think their class is the most important one. I didn't have that much trouble with any of them. I worked hard, but not any harder than I had to. I don't take homework home at all. I usually end up with pretty good grades, so why kill myself, you know? I have about a ninety-one average this year. I can't like it. It seems senseless.

*

You know, ever since Jason killed himself, they ask how you are. If you just have an off day, it's "How are you? You doin' okay?" It's not like you're thinking of slitting your wrists or anything. But they don't care, really, and don't treat kids like adults.

CHAPTER 3

"Hello in There": Taking College into the Community

"HELLO IN THERE"

In 1970, I began work on the Ph.D. in order to keep my job. I was twenty-eight. In the summer of 1979, I completed my dissertation and was awarded the degree. I was thirty-seven. I had poured nine precious years of the only life I would ever have to live into—into what? Into a cistern. That's how it seemed to me—a dark, dank, empty place with no light and with nothing in it that light could illuminate except its emptiness. It seemed to me, in all those nine years, that there was absolutely nothing worth saving there, nothing worth treasuring, nothing worth being pleased enough about to make up for the loss, though I had done my best, my absolute best, to make those nine years meaningful.

Before that time, I had tried to believe that a Ph.D. meant something, meant that you had transcended knowledge, and found wisdom, transcended arrogance and found humility, transcended self-absorption and learned compassion. Oh, I know it was foolish to make such assumptions. I knew that at the beginning. It was just that I wanted to meet some of my elders and believe that they were wise, humble, and compassionate, and move nearer, myself, to what I wished they represented. What a disappointment it was to find that, in addition to arrogance and self-absorption, all that most of my elders seemed to have was information that they copied from their professors, who copied it from theirs, and so forth, back to the time of Milton and Dryden, or farther than that, to find that all they did was talk and talk and talk about this text or that, or this critic or that. To find that all I was expected to do was take awe-filled, or at least dutiful, notes on their second- or third-hand notes, while they themselves strutted around campus like the emperor in the children's story, without enough on, and without even a kingdom beyond the boundaries of their own imaginations.

The requirements for the dissertation summed up the absurdity of it: You must write something that is valuable and new, but you may only do it by supporting your thesis with references to the work of others who have gone before you—no matter how dull and how short-sighted and unenlightened those others might be.

It was a rite of passage, my colleagues insisted. So your professors have a chance to strut and bully and preen and say yea and nay. So your dissertation joins the rows of all the other identically bound black books with the fake gold writing on them, in a dark dead letter office in the library of your alma mater. They had gone through it. What's the big deal? People call you *doctor* now. You have the right to *insist* on it if you wish, to treat clerks in the university store, and in the stores downtown, as if they were your inferior. Provided that your colleagues promote you one of these decades, you can even serve on the Evaluation Committee and pass judgment on your peers. Think of it! Where else could you go? What else could you do—and be so impressed with yourself?

For a long time, it wasn't something I could laugh at, though the Monday after I received the degree, I felt almost light-hearted as I filled two thirty-three-gallon garbage cans with my professors' lecture notes and my drafts of course papers and dissertation chapters, and lay in the hammock on my back porch, waiting for Haney's Disposal Service to arrive and take it all away to the landfill, certain beyond all doubt that I would never ever teach any of it to any of my own students or refer to any of it ever again.

How did one grieve the loss of nine whole years? How did one gather those years in one's tired arms, like a child in a Diego Rivera painting gathered flowers, and offer them up to the goddess of experience and say, "I didn't see another way, I didn't see another way, I didn't see another way. Would that I had had the ability, the faith, the courage, the hope, the understanding, the sheer luck—to see!"?

I grieved as well as I could. I stood on my small shore and looked out as far as I could look—as everything I thought my thirties meant sailed beyond my eyes' reach. I stood looking at the empty water edge, stood listening to the bitter waves all around me, until I no longer knew where I ended and they began. I stood alone and tasted the complete sadness of my aloneness, and then did what I had intended to do nine years before: I walked over to the nearest nursing home with its familiar epigraph carved, large and indelible, above the door: "Abandon all hope, ye who enter," and asked if my students and I could "adopt" some of the patients and teach them some creative ways of looking at their lives.

I figured I understood something about their grief, knew it was very like mine, only larger and more irrevocable. I figured it would do my students some good to realize that in the real world, grades matter less than an ant's breath, and lives matter in ways beyond all measuring, and we ourselves could be agents of hope once we understood that. I figured we would call what we did our "Creativity Group," and we would show the patients that, even though we were young and naive and inexperienced and free, we knew how to listen, and wanted to listen, and had room for them in our world. I figured our listening would wash some windows in a place where windows meant a lot, where windows were everything, and where they had been neglected for more years, and more lifetimes, than we knew. I obtained permission to do this—to spend a month by myself first, walking up and down the halls of the nursing home, talking to anyone who would talk to me, and then to choose fifteen patients, residents, whom my college students would adopt, and work with, for the rest of the semester and, perhaps, the year.

What a blessing it was, to enter the lives of these people who, until then, had assumed that they had gone there to die. What a blessing it was—and what a relief—to discover how easy it was to know them, to encourage them, to be so encouraged by them, to make their day, to make ours.

In a week, I was "a regular." All those who sat in the patients' lounge, keeping a careful eye on the door, knew who I was, filled me in on the news since my last visit a day or so before. So and so had a birthday. So and so finished her ninety-first afghan, so and so's daughter came from Ohio, so and so's not working here any longer, so and so has a new roommate, so and so went to the hospital, so and so went to visit her family.

Every day I entered a new room, a new life, found out this one was from here, this one from there. This one had a farm just down from this place; that one lived all her life, just up from the such and such by the so and so, went to the Catholic church. All her relatives came from so and so, moved there in such and such year. When they were young, they used to, when they got married, they. Now they. Isn't it a shame that? Would you ever expect that? What do you do if? And how are? And did you know? And I always thought, but now I. And you know, they will never. And besides.

"Hello in there." Hello. What a simple and wonderful word. Hello to Evelyn, with both of her legs amputated above the knee. Hello to her pale pink nightgown, and her pale pink smile, and her kind and observant eyes, and her thoughtful and alert and genuine and engaged conversation. Hello to the Margaret with the heart problem, the Margaret full of mischief, the Margaret who was always dressed to go out the door, and who never went. Hello to Jean, her roommate, a nurse herself, who read books of all kinds, who read nursing magazines, who visited her family on Fridays and stayed till Sunday, who went to eat in restaurants, who knew what went on in the world outside. Hello to Angelo, who came over on the boat from Italy at the age of four, who remembered the trip, who remembered before that, remembered the almond tree outside his bedroom in Italy, who remembered picking almonds off the tree, who became a barber, who remained a barber all his life, who was ninety-four now, and who had not been outside the nursing home since the day he entered— except for once, when it frightened him so much that he asked to return immediately. Hello to the other Margaret whom the nurses lifted into a chair next to the foot of her bed, where she sat all day, a foot from her television, who had not left her room for a year. Hello to Mr. B., who had a room here, but who was not quite a resident, who had a room full of framed photographs he himself had taken, a room full of his own writing desk and bookcases and chairs, who had written his own books, who was ninety-one and hard of hearing, and who took singing lessons and who could play melodies on the piano. Hello to Mary, who had a stroke on her right side, whose right arm was covered with bruises that never healed, who cried in pain every time she was moved, who sank down, farther and farther into her chair, who could not help it, who was angry if anyone else got attention before she did, who let you know about it.

Hello to Bertha, who was one hundred and three, who walked, alone, down the long hallway, stooped over, slowly, her hand inching along the shiny chrome railing, who had outlived her husband and her three sons, and who was alone now, with only a granddaughter, who lived far away and who could not come to see her. Hello to Anna, who could not join my group because she was a farm woman with a sixth grade education, who had a nose bigger than Jimmy Durante's, who dared not to impose such a nose on all of us, who had a doctor who could not see beyond her nose and who charged her for an office visit, she said, every time he put his head in the door and remarked on it.

Hello to dozens and dozens more, up and down the long hallways, on two floors, where nobody but nurses and cleaning ladies walked most days, until the cooks came up in the elevator with breakfast, with lunch, with supper, with the three high points of the day.

Hello to the staff, with their movies about places these people would never travel, with their bright little singsong voices asking how *are* we today, Bertha and Margaret and Angelo and Mary and Anna and Eleanor and Evelyn, with their elementary school valentines and shamrocks and their little black silhouettes of Washington and Lincoln, and their little construction paper signs outside the rooms, and their little programs, and their little balloon exercises for patients in wheelchairs and their little ways of treating adults as if they were all in preschool, as if they were all as undeveloped as apple blossoms, as if they all never had a life that was just as real and just as important and just as interesting and just as absorbing and just as hard to let go of and to move on from as their lives are, and will be.

Hello to all of you who wept real tears about the food, about the way people here treated you, about the pain you felt, about the loneliness you felt, about the fear you felt, about the dying that you did not want, that you did not want for a thousand years, about the homes that you would never see again, about the families who never came to visit, and who never called, and who never sent cards, and who went on without you, as if you had already died.

Hello to all of you, and thank you, thank you, thank you, for being what you were, and for giving me and my students a chance to be part of your lives.

THE "COMBINE"'LL GETCHA, IF YOU DON'T WATCH OUT!

It was Friday afternoon. Those of us who had chosen to be in the "Creativity Group" at the nursing home sat in a large circle, student/patient, student/patient, around the room. I had instructed the students to repeat an exercise we had done in class: "Ask your partner to tell a story he or she likes to remember. Take notes verbatim. Try to capture your partner's *voice*. To do that, write down the slang, the mispronounced words, the cut-off endings, everything—exactly as he or she speaks. It is not *data* we are seeking; it is the spirit of your partner—her character, her feeling unlike any other feeling, a moment in his life unlike any other moment, any other life."

The only difference, this time, was that many of their partners could not hear them if they spoke in their normal voices. They needed to sit close, look at their partners' faces, find out if they were coming across. They needed to listen more than they talked, needed to concentrate on listening, needed to ask real questions, questions they wanted to know the answers to, questions that helped them understand. They needed to draw their partners out until they could picture what they wanted them to picture.

They did this—created a room full of excited, cheerful talk, two by two by two by two, all around the room, not one person who was not engaged, not one person who was left out, who was not talking or listening. Their partners told of the time they got spanked for crawling under a train at the age of four, ninety-six years ago, told about going to the fair, eating hot sausage sandwiches with peppers and onions, funnel cake, cheesecake, ice cream, all in the same day, told about learning to be a barber, told about nursing school, told about walking through the park to church. Their lives came back, their lives felt real. My students read their stories back to them, loudly, clearly, enthusiastically, magically created those times again.

There was no sign of depression, no sign of tears, no sign of death. We were all in the moment, we were all having a discussion that counted for something—for all of us.

The director of the nursing home called me into her office while the others continued their discussion. She said she was sorry, but our project could not continue after all. It was too disturbing to the residents.

They were, after all, used to a quieter lifestyle, used to silence, used to order. Such excitement would raise their blood pressure. They might die of excitement.

I looked at her, speechless, tears in my eyes. I was relieved now that I had read *One Flew Over the Cuckoo's Nest*, that I understood what Big Nurse was about, that I understood something about what institutions did to our spirits. I did my best not to punch any holes in the spotless windows, described how happy and engaged everyone had been as I left the room, explained how carefully I had prepared every patient and every student for this meeting, reminded her I had spent a *month* talking at length with each of the residents in the group, reminded her that I had earned their trust.

"I understand," Big Nurse said. "But we must do what is best for the patients." I guessed Kesey had visited this town, had stood where I was standing, had heard what I heard.

"How about a counterproposal?" I asked. "Suppose we get together once a month as a group, and the rest of the time, the students visit their adopted person alone, one to one? Really, one hour a month wouldn't be too much of a strain on them, would it? It would just be part of an ongoing relationship. And I would continue to visit all of them so that they would all be used to me, would know me like a relative. How about it?" I tried to remain calm, to remove the urgency from my voice, my posture, act as if I were selling my old television in a classified ad. I stuffed my hands in my pockets, looked out the window, gave her time to decide.

"Okay," she said, at last. "I guess that won't do any harm. I just want what's best for the residents."

"Sure," I answered. I hoped I didn't sound sarcastic. I nodded my head. "Thanks."

We continued. The students all visited, took small gifts, read to their adopted partners, talked about how their school days were going, listened to stories about the farms, the towns, the births, the marriages, the deaths their partners wanted to talk about, examined the afghans they were knitting and the baby blankets they were crocheting and the plants they were growing in the window, and found their own ways to create and build their friendships.

Meanwhile, I asked all the patients, one at a time, what we should change if we could change only one thing about the nursing home.

Every one of them said, "The food!" I asked what food they would most like to eat. They all said, "Pizza!" I introduced myself to the cooks, told them this story, and explained that I had a plan. I imagined the patients forming an assembly line, making pizza from scratch, everyone doing a small task. I had already talked to two who were willing to make the dough in their room and let it rise on a shelf over the radiator. I could bring bowls, mixing spoons, flour, yeast, everything we needed—if they would just bake the pizza during our session while we wrote poems for an hour. They readily agreed to help.

The day of the pizza revolution came. I had a task for everyone. This one rolled out the dough. These two placed it in the pan. This one opened the can of tomato sauce. This one poured it in. This one added herbs. This one added a little salt. This one added pepper. This one grated cheese.

When I walked in, the staff introduced me to a new resident they had decided to add to our group. The new person loudly complained that she did not want to come, that she was a cripple, that she obviously could not do anything. She said that they had forced her to be here against her will. She had arthritis. Her legs lay on a platform, parallel to the floor. They looked thin, frail, useless, just as she said. Her fingers were swollen and deformed. She was wearing pajamas, looked like she belonged in bed. No one else in the group was wearing pajamas.

I had gone over and over the tasks, had made sure that each person could do what I had arranged. I stared at her. "Please," I said to myself. "*Think* of something for this woman!"

"How's your *mouth*?" I asked her.

She stopped complaining and looked at me. "You can see there ain't nothing wrong with my *mouth*!" she said.

"Good!" I told her. "Then suppose we put the bowl of sauce in your lap! You steady it with your hands and watch to be sure that everybody does his or her task right. It will be a big help to us."

The shiny aluminum bowl went in her lap. Everyone gathered around her. Everyone did what he was asked to do. The students gathered close, watched, grinned, encouraged, applauded, as if their partners were the hometown team. "That's *it*, Angelo! Good for *you*, Bertha. All *right*, Margaret. Good, look at that! Boy, that smells good. What a beautiful crust! Wow, I can hardly wait!"

The cooks stood watching. They applauded too, offered to hire the residents to work for them, and whisked our pizza into the kitchen. While we wrote our poems and stories, we smelled tomato sauce and yeast dough, talked excitedly about what we had just done, cheered when the cooks returned. Everybody had a slice. One resident leaned her head back, held her pizza slice in the air above her, and slowly lowered it into her mouth. Food was food again. Who would have thought it possible? This was our fishing trip. The patients had their dignity back, their courage, their confidence, their hope. We could cook something else another time. We could have real food. We could die later, and maybe die a little happier. But, right now, we were going to *live*.

I announced that on Saturday, Mary, Evelyn, and I were going to make peanut butter cookies; anyone who wished could join us. Mary, the grouchy, jealous one, paralyzed on one side, would use her good hand, be our "masher." Evelyn would measure the ingredients. I would stir them.

On Saturday, the new woman was there too. "I thought it might help my fingers if I rolled the dough into balls," she said. "I used to make peanut butter cookies. Now turn my chair so my back is to you. I don't want anybody watching." She formed all the balls of dough. Mary mashed each one with the fork, criss-cross. The cooks were ready for us, loved what we were doing. We distributed cookies to our group. They were delicious, crisp, fresh, warm—just like home.

A month later, the whole group tried pierogies. This time, no one was wearing pajamas. Our newest member had called her daughter, asked her to bring slacks. She was going to try physical therapy, she told her. Maybe she'd be able to walk. It was worth a try.

My students were writing about these things. They talked about the patients all the time, couldn't get over how exciting it was to go there, to know the patients, to get rid of their stereotypes of nursing homes, of "old people," to bring so much encouragement to people they had never met before.

Some of my colleagues rolled their eyes in disgust at this project, told me I should be creating scholars, not Florence Nightingales.

"These are people," I told them, "who hated writing, who made hundreds of mechanical errors at the beginning of the semester, who had no interest in reading, who never went to the library, who were afraid of it, who were afraid to confront their ignorance and their fear. They are not afraid now. They write thoughtfully and clearly, with a real voice. They talk about real things, in a way that clearly matters to them. They know what dialogue is. They practice it week after week. They aren't trapped in shallow, phony monologues. Isn't that encouraging? Isn't that wonderful? Isn't that enough for one semester?"

"No," many of them said. "No. If that's all they're capable of, then they're not college material, and they don't belong in college."

BEYOND DEGREES

The semester ended. The students went home for the summer. I asked older students, faculty, and a few middle school students to help me with the Creativity Group in the nursing home. Most of the faculty I asked said they didn't want to go. Nursing homes were too depressing; they smelled like urine. They didn't want to think about things like that. Most of the time now, I went alone.

One day, as I entered the building, I heard the oldest member of our group screaming at an aide. Never had she done such a thing! I listened outside her door in disbelief. She was screaming, "You will pay! You will pay! You will pay!"

I went in, leaned down next to her good ear. "It's Nancy," I said. "What's wrong? What's the matter?"

She continued to scream, "You will pay!"

"She's been doing this every day about this time," the aides said as they left. "Every day this week."

I spoke loudly, firmly, into her ear: "Listen! I don't know what's happened. I want to understand. I understand that you are very unhappy about something."

"You *know*!" she said, just as firmly.

"I *don't* know," I answered. "I wish I did. But I'll go home now, and think about it, and then I'll come back tomorrow, and we can talk. Is that okay?"

She stopped screaming, looked at me. "Yes," she said. "Do that."

"Okay," I said. I held her hand in both of mine, then left.

I had walked about twenty feet away from the nursing home when I realized that I *did* know what must have happened: she must have refused to eat. She must have told the aides that she wanted to die, and the staff must have force-fed her. I almost turned and retraced my steps, but decided to wait, let her rest, and return the next day as I had promised.

The next day I leaned down, spoke into her good ear, as I always did, and said what I always said. "Are you *there*?" I asked.

"Yes," she said, as she always did, "*I'm* here."

"Listen," I told her. "I thought about what you were so unhappy about yesterday, and I think I know what it is. Do you want me to say?"

"Yes," she said.

"I think that you told the staff that you didn't want to eat, that you wanted to die, and I think they said they couldn't allow that, and they had to force-feed you."

She looked at me, tears in her eyes. She sobbed and sobbed. "Yes," she said. "That's exactly what happened. Why can't I die? Why can't the Lord take me? What have I done to deserve this?"

"Maybe, before you die," I told her, "you're supposed to have a friend visit you, so you don't have to die so lonely. That wouldn't be hard for me. I can visit. I can come every day around at least one of your meals, and I promise I won't force you to eat. I'll leave it up to you to tell me when you want to. And we'll just talk—about whatever it is you want to talk about."

This was what we did for a year. For two weeks, she said nothing about eating, and neither did I. And then one day she said, "I'm hungry."

I almost thought I had imagined it. "Say it again," I told her. She did. I hurried into the kitchen, broke the news to the cooks, asked for some chicken bouillon and some jello. We found some. She sipped the bouillon, had a bite or two of jello, and said that was enough. I stopped. After that, she told me she was hungry at every visit. I fed her. We talked about her memories, about the relatives who had died, about the way they had lived, about the life she had had with her husband, about how handy she used to be around the house after he died. It took maybe two hours for her to eat and talk. I told myself I was not in a hurry, told myself that whatever I was going to do afterward could wait.

She gained weight. Her arms became muscular. She showed me her grip. She smiled. She laughed. The staff told me she had not screamed since the day I first spoke with her. They wondered what I said. I said she had been lonely and had wanted to die, but now she had changed her mind.

A year later, I came into her room. Her eyes were closed, as they often were. I spoke into her ear, as I always did. "Are you *there*?" I asked. "*No*," she said.

I wrapped my hands around her hand, sat down, said nothing. The next day, she was turned on her side with her knees drawn up. I rested my hand on her shoulder and did not speak. She died, sleeping, at the end of the week.

I told my new students about these visits, told them how our class, in an earlier semester, had visited all these patients, had become part of their lives, had written their compositions about them. They told me about equally real experiences from their own lives. It seemed to them, too, that schools were too far removed from the "real world," that there was no place where they could talk, and think, and write about what mattered most to them. School, outside their major, they agreed, was not about what mattered. It was about checking off requirements on a list. It was about going through motions to get the degrees they needed for the jobs they wanted. And they could not see how schools, as a whole, could be any different.

PLEASE LIVE

In a dream, my friend stood next to me with a gun in his hand. Terrified, I asked what he was doing. He told me I *knew* what he was doing. I pleaded with him to *live*. "Please *live!*" I said. "Please!" He looked away from me, shot himself, fell to the floor dead. I tried to scream. No sound came out. I woke up, tears streaming down my face.

Please live! Please live! Please live! It never occurred to me that this is what being an English professor would be about. It was not what I had studied in college. It was not what any professor of mine had ever talked about. Yes, two of my favorite professors had died of cancer, and two others had had family members who were terminally ill, and, yes, their lives had been centered around their own and their loved ones' dying. How could they not be? But these people, all of them, wanted to *live*—not just endure, not just exist, but *be* and *do* what mattered to them most for as long as they could. I didn't understand. I didn't know words to say what I was beginning to realize. I wished I did not have to realize it. I wished I could go on as usual, thinking about where to go for dinner, or what to have, thinking about oil changes and department meetings and whether this candidate or that would rock our little departmental dinghy, whether this one or that should row.

It was eight o'clock on a blue-sky morning in the summer. I was in my composition class on the second floor of the humanities building, passionately explaining the difference between mechanical, dutiful writing and writing that meant something to the writer. I was saying that a trusting relationship had to exist, had to be built between the teacher and the student if writing were to be valuable at all. I was saying that the teacher could not do this alone, could not create such a relationship alone, that it took each of us. Twenty-five of us were sitting in a circle around the edge of the classroom. The slight breeze floating in through the open window above the coat rack was already warm. It smelled like a mixture of dry, warm pine needles and freshly cut grass.

The center of the room was empty, except for a few unused chairs. A boy about four seats to my right was sound asleep. I stopped talking, looked at him for a while, wondered if I should wake him, decided not to, told myself he was probably out late last night, was probably not a morning person. I went on talking.

A boy about ten seats to my left, under the window, suddenly began to laugh. His laugh was loud, hysterical. It got louder and louder. I glanced at him. Several students looked over at him. Some looked at their laps. The sleeping student did not waken. I looked at the laughing student, saw that he was not looking at me, saw that he was absorbed in something that was not in the room. No one else in the class was laughing. I stopped talking, sat in silence, and waited for him to be done laughing. He continued. I felt, suddenly, briefly, hurt. Maybe he was laughing at the idea that I wanted the class to be meaningful. I called him by name, asked if he wished to say something. He looked at me at last. "No," he said, matter-of-factly, shaking his head. He laughed again, louder, longer. I continued listening to his laugh, waiting. Finally, I decided to go on without him.

I leaned forward, spoke as distinctly as I could, spoke quietly, to the rest of the class, as if this laughing boy were not there, went on with what I had been saying. They had to strain to hear me over his laughter.

"This is ludicrous," I thought, but I went on. When he realized that I was going to continue, he quietly gathered his books and tiptoed out of the room. I listened as he turned the door handle.

"Does anyone know what that was about?" I asked the class. No one did.

Afterward, I asked other teachers what they might have done in my place. They would have motioned angrily toward the door and commanded "*Out!*" They would have removed him bodily, would have lectured him, would have failed him for disrespect. I did none of these things. When he was not in class the next day, I wrote him a note, said it hurt to have the class interrupted in this way, said I felt that there was something there that I needed to understand, and asked if he would be willing to come to my office privately and talk about it or write me a note in reply. He did both.

He told me that just before coming to class, he had received a phone call informing him that a friend had been in a motorcycle accident. He was in the hospital in critical condition—in another city several hours away. He had tried several times to call the hospital, but could not find out how his friend was, so he had decided to go to class. Once he was there, however, he could think of nothing else. He had heard me say what I had said about trust. He had seen the boy across the room from him sleeping, had understood that I had been talking about something that mattered to me, as his friend mattered to him, and had felt how strange and lonely it was when what mattered most to you mattered not at all to other people. And then he had begun laughing his eerie, helpless, terrified, grieving laugh.

In another semester, three of my students told me they were seriously considering suicide. One wrote a composition about an illness that prevented him from having sex. He said he felt that his life was meaningless without it, and he didn't know what to do. Because of the illness, he could die at any time. He couldn't tolerate the anxiety of anticipating his own death and the anguish of realizing that he might never have the chance to live out his life. Another wrote a composition about the violence in his home and his recent attempt to stop it by standing in front of one parent when the other one pulled out a gun. He said it "worked" that time, but he was terrified by the possibility that it could happen again, and again, and again. His only salvation had been to leave the house and go for long walks in the dark, but last night he found himself walking in a cemetery. He thought he saw a ghost there. He strangled it—and then realized, to his horror, that he had killed a small, white dog. Another student wrote a composition about how afraid she was to be alone with herself "for fear of what she might do." She didn't know anyone she could turn to for help.

When I read their compositions, I invited these students to come to my office and talk more about what was going on in their lives. I explained that I was not trained in psychology, that I was only an English professor, only a fellow human being. But I could listen and maybe that would help. I explained that the campus counseling service was there for students who would like counseling and offered to provide names of counselors for them to call, offered to be with them as they called, or to make the call myself while they were with me. One made an appointment there, returned to my office afterward, and said she had changed her mind—she would feel more comfortable talking to *me* because, as she put it, the counseling service was *obligated* to listen to her, but I listened because I cared.

The others said they didn't want to go to the counseling center either, would rather talk to me as well.

I encouraged them to keep coming to class, to keep coming in to see me, and to consider asking for support from their friends and from the resident advisors in the dorms. Meanwhile, I called the counseling service myself, explained that I was not trained in counseling, asked that the counselor call the resident advisors and ask them to initiate some kind of supportive, welcoming conversation with the students. The counselor agreed to do that. He said that he, too, felt uneasy in the face of such deep emotional problems, said he had only superficial training in these areas. He spent most of his day helping students plan study schedules.

We limped through the semester in this way. All three students remained in the class, stayed caught up on their work, talked with me all semester long, disappeared at the end of the semester and never came back to talk or to tell me they were okay.

The students in the ten-year project were in the sixth grade now. Some of the sixth grade girls were dating high school boys, boys with cars, boys with criminal records. Other girls lined up outside the middle school door after school and screamed "Slut!" and "Pig!" at them as they walked by. "She's a slut!" they hollered. "There goes the little slut!"

These girls tried not to cry. They tried to think of a way to get home without having to walk past their screaming peers. I told the principal about this, said that some of the students I worked with there were hurting very badly. He said he knew that. I told him that they needed to be able to scream and beat on things, do something physical with their hurt and anger. He agreed, but said that there was no place in school where students could do that. I asked if I could take them outside—away from the school. He said yes. I took them to a restaurant in the middle of the day, where we filled a booth, ordered cokes, and talked. The next day, the principal said he was sorry, but there must have been a misunderstanding. Insurance regulations wouldn't allow this.

The girls told me how much they wanted to have babies.

Babies, they said, would love them and need them. They told me how unsympathetic their parents were, how out of touch their parents were, how out of touch their teachers were, how out of touch everybody was, how boring school was, how far away the future was, how painful and frightening it was to be called a slut. I gave one girl a ride home from the other side of the building so she didn't have to walk by the name-callers and suggested that her father pick her up after school for a while. He did.

On the day before her birthday, I stopped at the local florist's and asked him to deliver one pink rose to her the next day. He did. She never received it. On her birthday, she went upstairs to her room and swallowed all the Midol tablets she had. She was too afraid to go downstairs and tell her father what she had done. Instead, she called a friend and told her. "Wow!" the friend said, and hung up. Finally, she told her father, and he took her to the hospital. From the hospital, she wrote to me, told me what she had done, and said "if it wouldn't be too much trouble," she would like to come and talk to me after she got out.

One student told me there used to be a suicide club composed of sixth grade girls who wanted to kill themselves. Another said they didn't really want to kill themselves. They wanted to live. They just wanted to feel hopeful. They just wanted people to listen.

How could they come to understand that sometimes you need to ask people to listen, because, many times, grown-ups have forgotten how painful and lonely they used to feel when they were in middle school?

Grown-ups tell themselves instead that kids today have nothing to complain about, have it easy, get everything handed to them. How could they come to understand that you have to break through that—break through that, if you can, when your pain is still small and temporary, so it doesn't get so large?

More than anything in the world, one said, she would like to have a baby. She wondered what I thought of this. I told her that a baby would be a wonderful thing to have. I said that all my adult life I had wanted one very badly too, and that was why, since I was single, I had decided to "adopt" her and the rest of her class and stay with them for ten years, until they were old enough to live on their own. That was the way I had handled it. I had decided not to have just one child. I had decided to have thirty. But if she had decided to have just one, I said, then the thing to do was to celebrate that decision, because a baby was a very beautiful and wonderful thing. I told her that, therefore, I would like to help her celebrate this decision by taking her out to lunch at a nice restaurant. She giggled and agreed to come. We set a date for the next week. I told her to dress up a little and promised that I would too.

I picked her up, drove her to the restaurant, smiling, laughing, doing my best to treat her as if she were not twelve. As we sat in my favorite booth near the window, looking over the menu, I asked her what she wanted—a boy or a girl. "Sh-h-h-," she said. "Somebody might *hear* you!" I suggested that after lunch we walk to the nearest children's shop and look at baby clothes. We did that, looked carefully at everything for newborns, examined colors, styles, price tags, thought about what else she would need to be sure this baby was safe and comfortable and had a good start in life. She spoke in whispers. We meandered through the store, talking about how neat babies were and how many skills it took to take care of them, and then I drove her home, waved good-bye, and told her to keep me posted.

A month later, she called. "Guess *what!*" she said excitedly.

"What?!" I asked. It was *my* turn to whisper.

"I got a *kitten*," she said. "Want to come over and see it?"

READING

There are always poems I do not get, allusions splattering under the tires of old habits, assumptions, roads I have not traveled or glanced at in the underbrush. Sometimes even freeways evade my attention. I am always looking at the ground nearest my feet, hoping not to trip on rocks or grains of sand, not to slip in snow, mud, wet grass, illusions. I am always looking at the sky, heaping up the tumbling white and gray treasures that slide, roll, swirl along the track of the horizon without colliding. (My mother used to say they would, and often did, collide. I never knew how she knew, and wanted to see for myself how they slammed into each other, rose limping, ambled away like two grizzlies equally matched, marking the same territory.)

But students so often missed what they missed for different reasons. Sometimes they slept all semester, partied long and laboriously, grieved that their youth was slipping away, dreaded the day that they would wake up with a spouse, a mortgage, children who resembled them, a nine-to-five job with all the excitement of a northern Nevada highway.

Students said they read. They read whatever was assigned, read it once, counting all the times they raided refrigerators, went out for pizza, took a shower, nodded over the book, stretched out full-length on the bed, distracted themselves with their favorite CDs. Many of them did not distinguish between fact and intention, so could not, of course, recall what their eyes had passed over en route to these other, far more appealing, destinations.

Sometimes I didn't know how to teach these students. I told them I didn't, asked them if there was something they wanted to learn, something they might like to read that I could order through the bookstore. They looked at me as if I were dressed in green fur with purple spots. "Whatever," they said. Some doodled on their desks, on the covers of their spiral notebooks.

"Well, in that case," I would say, "I need your help if I'm to teach you anything worth learning. Please take a moment and draw with stick figures a picture of the universe with both you and me in it, and with the rest of our class in it." They would rub their eyes, stretch, search in their backpacks for a pen. I would ask them to divide into groups of four or five, examine each other's drawings, choose one that best described their situation, and nominate someone in their group to reproduce the drawing on the board. They would be alert now. Some would be laughing. Some would be afraid that their drawings would anger me. I would reassure them. I would not be angry. I was just curious, mystified. I wondered if their parents realized how expensive tuition was these days.

One semester, the board was filled with stick figures. Dr. Gill was standing on Pluto; the entire class was together, on the earth. Dr. Gill was standing on the other side of a wide river; the entire class was huddled in a group on this side. There was no ferry, no bridge. The students were not looking at Dr. Gill. They were laughing, talking, looking at each other, lounging in the sun, having a beer party. Several had drawn two groups of students, labeled one group "normal," the other group "nursing majors."

We focused on an elaborate drawing of Australia, where all the students were gathered. Dr. Gill was standing on the Great Barrier Reef. One student was in a boat, rowing back and forth between the Barrier Reef and Australia through "shark-infested waters." We discussed the shark-infested waters, confessed that knowledge that mattered was frightening, especially when you realized that once you started opening yourself up to learning, you couldn't always control what you learned, and some of those learnings would cause you pain that you could not easily erase or dismiss. Some kinds of pain could kill you, could kill your naiveté, your hope, your good mood, could make you question your parents, your own motives, your relationships, your career choices, your political beliefs, your religion.

No one knew how Dr. Gill got to the Great Barrier Reef. It was very beautiful there—pure blue water, fish gliding in and out of the coral formations. She saw so much beauty that other people took for granted. But the Great Barrier Reef was uninhabitable. No human beings lived there. How was it that she could survive there, by herself? Clearly, the rest of the class did not want to go there, did not want to risk seeing what she saw. And she had no boat. Perhaps she swam back and forth through these same waters, risked her life to show people the beauty she saw. But she couldn't show anybody anything if no one would accompany the solitary student in the boat. The only solution was for him to shuttle her over to Australia. There was no other way to have a class.

After this lesson, Dr. Gill packed her bags and accepted a ride to Australia. The class talked about how to tell if sharks were really in the water or if those ominous fins belonged to something else. She unrolled some manuscripts she had carried with her, through all waters, and asked students to create some manuscripts of their own, adaptations, sometimes, of hers. Her manuscripts included Ernest Hemingway's

short story, "A Clean, Well-Lighted Place," James Baldwin's, "Sonny's
Blues," the poems of Langston Hughes, and poems written by women
and children from many countries.

"Don't worry," she said, "if you don't understand everything you
read. Why would that be necessary? Who exists that understands everything he or she reads? The authors themselves sometimes see new
meanings in their old works—or maybe never look at them again.
Some go on to open up new confusions, search for new paths through
whatever terrain they feel compelled to move into."

They didn't know this, they said. And they thought whoever had the
most answers got an A. Even now, they were not sure it was safe to
speak their solitary minds. How could they get over the fear of scaring
themselves? They wished, now, that there *were* just one right answer to
every problem, a teacher's guide they could memorize for the test. How
do you grade, then, if there are more answers than we all know, than we
can all search for in one semester, or one life?

There was nothing else to measure, Dr. Gill said, but the carefulness
and the sincerity of our examination. It was encouraging to know that
others were willing to try to see, to try to listen, to try to subtotal, to say
where they were, to trace some of their route, to show the rest of us how
they arrived there. She was only a guide, she said. And not the only
guide. She was not the owner of the property, had no deed, no measure
of the circumference, no radius, did not know the center, could not, herself, see where they were capable of going, could see only where they
had thought of going, or had been, could see only through her own lens.
But she had been back and forth to the Great Barrier Reef, could bear
witness to some of its treasures, could find treasures almost anywhere,
at her feet, in her own hands. There would be treasures at their feet. Or
maybe just some broken shells. But how could we know, if we didn't
bend down and look?

They looked at Hemingway, as so many readers before them had
looked. They, too, heard the older waiter say that the younger one had
"everything," had "youth, confidence, and a job," heard the younger one
tell him he had everything too, heard him say no, he was not young, and
he never had confidence. They understood how "nothing" might be both
an absence and a presence, saw where our discussion was headed, were
willing to ask why the old man killed himself, why the older waiter

wanted to keep the café open, why you could not "stand before a bar with dignity," why the older waiter couldn't sleep (Hemingway 1961, 32). They scrutinized the café, the street, the bodega across the street, they looked from the younger waiter to the older waiter to the old man, tried to see what Hemingway might have missed, accepted that they might not be able to see where the nothing came from, or what used to be there in its place, but acknowledged that this story did not take place off the coast of Australia, that it took place every day, much closer to home.

They read through most of Baldwin's story easily enough, sympathized with the older brother, sympathized with Sonny, felt for their father, their mother, had some idea of the roads they had traveled, the weight of their losses, the fragility of their hopes. They struggled with the ending, where Sonny played the piano, and his older brother tried his best to listen, and to hear. They had not ever thought of music in this way, but thought of it in this way now.

SEE WHAT?

> "And when did we see thee sick or in prison and visit thee?"
>
> Matthew 25:39

A friend of mine was a minister who preached about his own learnings. I liked that, and often went to his church on Sunday to listen to what he had to say. I walked in one morning, and as I sat down, an elderly, gossipy woman I did not know leaned toward me, whispering loudly: "Did you see *that*?"

"See *what*?" I whispered back.

She looked across the aisle, a few rows ahead of me. I looked. I saw a young girl, who might have been fourteen, a defiant, sullen, angry, tough, street-wise girl, dressed in unmatched, faded, too-small, wrong-season Salvation Army clothes. She was sitting in the pew, holding a baby that might have been six months old. I met her eyes for a second, and looked away.

"She dropped her baby on the *floor!*" the older woman said.

I looked again, and looked away. That night, I dreamed about this girl. I was standing with her, looking at her face. I saw everything I had already seen. I saw this girl's hopeless, helpless, desperate, angry defiance. In the dream, I was crying. Waking, I realized that I could not go back to that church, could not sit there in a pew, could not listen to any sermons—no matter how thoughtful and thought-provoking, unless I intervened in this girl's life. I could not be the one who said, "Did you see *that*?" And I could not see, and say "That's too bad," and walk away.

The next day, I went to the minister, told him my dream, and asked if I might know her story. Her name was Sarah. She was retarded. Her mother had died when she was in elementary school. She had had two children before, both of whom had been taken away. Now the local officials were trying to take her third child away. She was scheduled to go to court soon about the child's custody. Everyone knew about her. Everyone knew what an unfit mother she was, knew she carried the baby up and down the street every day, knew that she fed her Kool-Aid in a baby bottle, knew that, once, in a restaurant, she had tried to give her stromboli.

Why did she drop the baby in church? He didn't know.

The next Sunday, I arrived early, stopped by the minister's office to say hello, and found the hallway packed with onlookers, Sarah screaming at him, crying. Her daughter had been put in a foster home. I walked calmly into the center of the crowd and asked the minister if he would like me to talk to her so he could begin the service. "I wish you would," he said. He gave me the key to his office. I introduced myself to her and guided her toward the office. "Let's talk," I said. "Let's figure out what we can do." She stopped screaming, walked with me. I closed the door as the prelude began.

I asked her if she would like to sit at the minister's desk. She would. She thought that was great—such a big, dark, highly polished, fancy desk. She had never sat there before. She swirled in the seat, grinned. I grinned too and sat down in a chair next to her. Suddenly, she was having an epileptic seizure.

I knew next to nothing about epilepsy, but remembered well the time a fellow college student had died in a grand mal seizure, and the time one of my own students had had a grand mal seizure in the back of the classroom. This was not a grand mal seizure.

Not sure what to do, I slowly guided her head down so it was resting on her folded arms on the desk. I gently rubbed her shoulders and her back and continued talking quietly to her. "That's okay," I said. "That's okay. It'll be all right. It'll be all right."

In a few minutes, she relaxed, cushioned her head on her arms, and remained that way. I continued to rub her shoulders and asked her if she felt better. She told me that that was the first time ever that she was not unconscious during a seizure, told me she had seizures all the time, had them on the street, fell to the sidewalk, was full of cuts and bruises. She said no one ever stopped to help her. They all walked around her and kept on going. Nobody even called the doctor. When she came out of a seizure, she found a telephone, called a taxi, and asked the driver to take her to the emergency room.

She told me she had had seizures since she was in second grade, when her sister accidentally hit her on the head with a baseball bat. She was twenty-four now. She lived by herself in a motel for transients, the only woman there. She paid her rent and kept all her receipts, but the landlord had accused her of being behind on payments and had threatened to evict her. She had her receipts in her purse now, and carried them everywhere with her so she wouldn't lose them.

I asked her if she could read. Yes, she could. She could read the newspaper. She found a newspaper, read it to me. And she could write, too.

I asked her what she had eaten that day. She had no stove, no hot plate, and no refrigerator. She didn't have a washcloth or a towel. She had canned goods, but no can opener. Every day she made herself a cup of instant coffee with hot water from the faucet. That was all she had had to eat that day. I asked her to come back to the church the next day, promised to be there, asked her to bring a list of everything she had eaten in the last week, told her I would like to show it to the minister. She agreed to do that.

The next day, she was there half an hour early. We went over the list. I put a star by foods that were healthy, put a minus by foods that weren't. She laughed. Most of the foods on her list were on the minus side. I asked her to come back in a week with a new list, and see how many stars she could get. She did. She had a lot of stars that time. She was calm, quiet, pleased with herself.

This was the beginning of a long, hard year for both of us. A good friend of mine was dying of cancer several hundred miles away. The minister was transferred to another congregation. I was a full-time college professor with over a hundred students. "My kids," as the students in the ten-year project were called, were in high school. Two of my college classes were three-hour evening classes. But Sarah's custody case was coming up, and I offered to go to court with her. I asked her what she thought would be best for the baby. She cried, looked at me, shook her head, and said she knew that it would be best for the baby if she were adopted by her foster family. It was just that, it was just that, it was just that . . .

I asked her if she had a lawyer. She did. I called the lawyer, explained that I was working with her, and told him what she had told me. He was understanding, said we could take our time. The baby was already in foster care. There was no rush. We could wait until Sarah was ready to voluntarily give her up. I asked if we could meet with him together, if he would explain this to Sarah just as calmly as he had explained it to me. We could do that. She must understand that, once she signed the papers, she could not change her mind.

I called my hairdresser, described Sarah, said that I would like to bring her in to have her hair cut and styled in a soft, curly, casual style. I explained that she had epilepsy, that she might have a seizure. I said it would help her a lot if her environment remained calm. I asked Sarah if she would like this. She would. She would love it. Afterward, I took her picture, showed her off to people she knew. She looked nice; she looked pretty. She smiled at herself in the windows we passed.

I called my doctor, described her seizures, and asked if he would examine her, see if anything could be done. He was amazed. Her medication was far too strong. He adjusted it. The seizures that had been going on for more than fourteen years *stopped—stopped completely.*

We found a small apartment, went through the classified ads for a bed, a sofa, a chest of drawers, a kitchen table. We went grocery shopping. She moved in, was thrilled, had never had an apartment before.

I received a call from her boyfriend. They had had a fight. She had run away. She might have taken pills. I called the police. We went looking for her. I brought the police up to date on her story, told them how much she had learned, how much she had improved. Her boyfriend found her and called me. She had taken an overdose of something. He still did not know what, did not know how much. I told the police I was afraid she would panic if they came to take her to the hospital, and offered to take her myself. I asked her boyfriend and his family to come with us. She did not resist. We sat in the emergency room until three o'clock in the morning, when they admitted her, at last, and pumped her stomach. I went home, slept a few hours, and went to class.

A few months later, they had another fight. This time, the hospital called me, told me she was in critical care, and was unconscious. She had taken more pills this time and was on the exact edge between living and dying. There was only one person who could bring her out of it, they said. I needed to come. I needed to call to her as if she were asleep, as if she were just waking up in the morning. If I came, several times a day, and did that, perhaps for several days, there was a chance she would come out of it.

I went to the hospital between classes, held her hand, called to her, my Lazarus: "Hi, Sarah. It's *me*, Nancy. It's time to wake up—okay?" I sat for an hour, holding her hand, calling to her again and again, went back to campus, taught Composition, taught American Literature, taught Literature and the Real World. For two days, nothing happened. On the third day, her eyelashes moved. She was far away, but she heard me. She couldn't quite find where I was. The next day, she opened her eyes, looked at me, knew me.

"We had a fight," she said. I knew. "How's Michael?" she asked.

"He's fine. He said to say he's thinking about you."

I asked if she would like to write him a letter. She would. I had paper with me. She wrote that she was sorry.

Her relationship with Michael ended. The hospital had arranged for her to visit a counselor. She asked me to go with her. I went. The counselor did not mention the suicide attempt and chatted casually about the weather, about epilepsy, about the services the community provided. Sarah's hour was almost up. I interrupted. "Sarah is just getting out of the hospital after an attempt to end her life. I think she needs to talk about that." The counselor turned to Sarah and said in a high, artificial voice: "Oh, are we thinking of doing something *bad* to ourself?! In that case, I will have to call the psychiatric ward and have you admitted!" She turned abruptly and left the office. Sarah leaped up, flew toward the huge, open second-floor window. I saw, flew faster, got between her and the window, closed it, gently hugged her, told her we cared about her, we wanted her to heal. "Let me go!" she screamed. "Let me go!" I let her go. She ran out the door. The counselor returned, looked around for Sarah. I told her she had left; she did not want to be admitted to the psychiatric ward. I told her I must go to class now. I went.

I explained to the new minister that Sarah needed a support group, that I couldn't be her only support. Sarah agreed and said she would very much like a support group. After that, we met regularly as a group. She had half a dozen phone numbers now, knew that all these people knew her and cared about her and would be there for her. She did not threaten or attempt suicide again.

Local officials made one attempt to force her to give up custody of her child. As we sat outside the courtroom waiting, half a dozen cold and catty women gossiped with each other about her as if she were deaf. I slouched down in my seat, closed my eyes, and listened to everything they said. They didn't know me, had no idea that I was there as her support, talked openly about how they had tape-recorded her without her permission to show that she was, indeed, an unfit mother, talked openly about how unwisely she had behaved with the child. Her lawyer was not present. Someone came out and told us she was sorry, but there would not be time for this case today.

A few weeks later, Sarah called. She calmly told me that she was ready to sign the papers and asked when we could schedule the signing. I went with her to the lawyer's office.

Not long afterward, she began a new relationship, and she and the new boyfriend eventually married. Her life was not "fixed" by any means, but this crisis was past, and she felt able to go on.

During this year, she gave me written permission to look at her high school records. According to those records, she was *not* retarded. Her IQ was normal.

It is not possible to know if any of her suffering might have been avoided if the school had had the insight, the concern, the staff, and the facilities to treat her differently, so perhaps it is foolish to wonder. But she was a talkative and lively girl. She did not hesitate to tell her story to anyone who would listen. What if she had been placed with teachers who were capable of understanding her behavior, with guidance counselors who were capable of offering guidance? What if she had been medically evaluated regularly? What if someone had intervened after her first two children were born? Before they were born? Before they were conceived? After her mother died? Before her mother died? When she was put in Special Education? Allowed to leave school? Allowed to roam the streets year after year? Why was she a source of detached, irritated amusement for so many people for so long? Why, when she was so clearly unable to help herself, did no one—in the school, in the church, in the community, for twenty-four years, try to see beyond her surface and help her heal at least the worst of her wounds?

I cannot answer for others. They know, as I do, that there are more Sarahs in the world than anyone could count, that they all need more than any of us could give them, even if we wanted to give them everything we had for as long as we had it to give. They have crossed into territories they cannot easily retreat from, have made choices they cannot annul, have survived depths of chaos that the rest of us cannot imagine and would not want to imagine. In doing so, they have left us on shores inconceivably far behind them. But sometimes their orbit comes close enough to ours to enable, even require, us to see. And what we see is what Chief Bromden in *One Flew Over the Cuckoo's Nest* sees. We see the faces looming out of the fog. We see that they are all human faces. And they see that we see. Who, at such times, can turn their backs and walk away? I knew, this time, that I could not.

DON'T ASK *ME* TO BE CREATIVE

My college students said, almost without exception, that they were not creative. They told me this the first day of class. Even English majors said so. "I am not creative," they said. And what this meant was that I should not *ask* them to be creative. It was, after all, asking the impossible. Creativity was for other people, for people next door, for people who wanted to take chances, make fools of themselves, have F's on their papers.

"I saw a girl wearing red slacks," one boy said. "She was walking across campus. She was probably creative. She was weird. Nobody wears red slacks." There was a sudden, heavy, palpably uncomfortable silence in the room. "That was *me!*" said the girl two seats behind him. "And I am *not weird*! I happen to *like* red slacks!" It was the boy who was red now.

The girl in red slacks had never spoken in class before, had thought of herself as a shy person. From this day forward, her shyness was gone. She talked. She took on anybody. She had come back from the dead—come back to defend red slacks, defend her *self*, defend anything else that might need defending. Thanks to her, our whole class realized that there was a difference between a college and a shopping mall, between a transcript and an education, between creative and weird.

Most semesters, there were no red slacks. Students said their *professors* were not creative either; they were *boring*. They *lectured*. They lectured *all the time*. The student's job was to take notes.

Some students told me they slept regularly in their classes and their grade point averages were starting to suffer. What creative solutions could we come up with for this problem? One girl said she was failing Art for the second time, just because she couldn't stay awake during the seventy-five minute lecture.

I offered to accompany her to class and see if I could stay awake myself. In the small, attractive, freshly painted auditorium, I positioned myself where the student said she always sat, on the right side, in the back, near the radiator. I looked around, figured there must be two hundred students here, all of them with notebooks, all of them writing as fast and as uncreatively as they could.

I decided to try taking notes myself. I was a good note taker. When I was an undergraduate, my notes had been in great demand. Reading them, my friends said, was like being there. Better than being there, sometimes. The professor was showing slides. I didn't know these paintings. I sketched the slides, found this fun, challenging. I sketched fast, without looking at the paper. Here's a slide. Notice X. Notice Y. Click. Now another. Notice D. Notice M. Click. Notice B. Notice R. Click. Seventy-five minutes of this—without a single expression of excitement or interest on professor's or students' part—and never once a chance to turn to a neighbor, discuss X, Y, D, M, B, R. Have to go on, go on, hurry, hurry. Twenty minutes left, fifteen minutes, ten, five, whew! Hard to cover so much in so little time, yes sir! You have seventy-five minutes. You gotta cover it. It will all be on the test. Identify this, identify that. How many of this is that, where is this, when is that?

My drawings faded away half an hour before the professor stopped talking.

I took my notes to my own class, asked what notes the others had taken. None like mine. I asked how much they enjoyed art. Not at all. I asked how many would like to go to an art gallery, see without slides. None. It was just General Ed. They had heard this course was a piece of cake. It was no big deal. An A, a D, a C—what difference did it make? It wasn't in their major.

I asked how many famous artists or musicians had graduated from our college. I was pretty sure I already knew the answer. What if they themselves could be famous artists? Not likely, they said. Not likely. Artists were born. Artists must not have been born around here. Must be their genes just didn't have art in them.

How about writers? Writers were the same. They were never any good at commas and semicolons and all that, always got in trouble for using run-on sentences, for ending sentences with prepositions. What was a preposition, anyway?

In the 1960s, I received a copy of Richard Lewis's book, *Miracles: Poems By Children of the English-Speaking World* (Simon and Schuster 1966), as a gift, and bought the companion prose volume a few years later. I brought these to class the first week of every semester, brought, also, Betty Edwards, *Drawing On the Right Side of the Brain* (Tarcher/Putnam 1989), to show students that there was more to their brains than their schools knew.

I always felt so mischievous at the beginning of a semester—could hardly wait to have them tell me that they were not creative, and I should not expect creativity from them. It never seemed to occur to anyone that other classes might have shaken their fingers at me in this same sort of way, might have had this same reflex response. Students *never* seemed to anticipate that I might not take their word for these unfortunate circumstances, that I might challenge them anyway. But saying "I'm not creative," I have learned, is like saying "I'm a shy person." Uncreative and shy people expect sympathy: "Too bad! What a shame! Poor thing! Of course I won't expect anything of you!" After all, how could a total stranger question them?

Every semester, I *laughed.* I suggested that they put their heads on their desks, or doodle, take their shoes off, do whatever they wanted to do, as long as they were quiet. I was going to read to them. I was going to take them back to elementary school, back to when they never gave a thought to whether they were creative or not, back to when people were not divided into creative and uncreative. I told them not to worry about taking notes; I didn't give tests, wouldn't think of giving tests. I wanted to see what they remembered when they didn't have to remember anything.

I read "This is a Poem" by Hilary-Anne Farley, age 5, from Canada. "This is a poem about god looks after things:/ He looks after lions, mooses and reindeer and tigers,/ Anything that dies," she begins (Lewis 1966, 14). As I read those lines, a softness, a quietness, came across the class. Some leaned forward, their chins on their hands. "Mooses," someone said. "I used to say that!" They spoke almost in whispers. Some wiped tears from their eyes. I went on to Ethel Hewell, age 11, Philippines, "My poem":

> My poem is full of joy
> And full of hope.
> I love my poem.
> I enjoy reading it
> While I'm alone.
> I forget my sorrows and
> My happiness comes along (16)

I read what Adrian Keith Smith, a four-year-old from New Zealand, had to say about how rain "screws up its face/and falls to bits" (56). I read how Gordon Lea, age 11, learned to whistle:

> . . .It was in Spring, and new sounds were all around.
> I was five or six and my front teeth were missing,
> But I blew until my cheeks stuck out.
>
> I remember walking up and down the block,
> Trying to impress those that heard me
> With the tunes and sounds that came from my mouth,
> For I sounded much better than the birds in the trees.
>
> I remember being hurt, for nobody seemed to care,
> And then I met an old man who stopped and smiled.
> He too blew until his cheeks stuck out.
> He sounded just like me, for his front teeth were missing (67).

I read ten-year-old Brian Andrews's poem about doors:

> The doors in my house
> Are used every day
> For closing rooms
> And locking children away (166).

And eleven-year-old Susan Morrison's: "Hours are leaves of life/ and I am their gardener . . . / Each hour falls down slow" (121).

I read ten-year-old Ken Dickinson's poem, "Raindrops":

> Raindrops shimmer down dirty glass
> And measle the window pane.
> The raindrops glide—leaving a motionless road.
> Raindrops fall breaking themselves to tiny china
> and run away like blood (58).

I read for at least half an hour, sometimes the entire period if students wanted me to. There was not a person in the room that day who left thinking that children were not creative, who left thinking that children just wrote "cute" things to please teachers and get good grades. In Lewis's book, there was none of the "Now, boys and girls, let's all write a nice haiku poem about the rain," none of the usual la-de-dah, de-dah, de-dah, de-dah that often passes for poetry in our elementary schools. This was the real thing, and they knew it. And if these little kids, many of them less than half their age, could do it—well, maybe, maybe— they could take the leap of faith and try it too.

DRAWING

At the beginning of every class, I asked students to answer a few questions about themselves and then draw a picture of themselves doing something they would rather do than be in class. Most of them used stick figures and drew themselves sleeping, watching television, drinking beer with their friends, or lying on a beach. They apologized for their lack of artistic ability, laughed at their drawings, showed them to each other. Later, I followed Betty Edwards's approach (*Drawing On the Right Side of the Brain* 1989) and taught them contour drawing. I told them, as so many art teachers probably have, that good drawing comes from an observant state of mind and is a byproduct of that state. I told them it was the same with essay writing, short story writing, poetry writing, but they were so used to writing for a grade, for a teacher, that they might not realize that, might not notice their mental states, might just write to get assignments done.

Pure contour drawing, as Betty Edwards explains and illustrates so well, is drawing the edges of something without looking at the paper—looking, then, only at the edges of the thing you are drawing, imagining that your hand is tracing the edges at the same slow rate your eyes are. Contour drawing made some students nervous. They rushed through the exercise, trying to get rid of their uneasiness. "Relax, play, warm up," I said. "Scribble, use your forearm, swirl around, feel the tension in your arm, in the joints of your fingers. Relax your hand, play with the way you hold the pencil. There's not one right way. Draw this face vase, profile of young girl, facing east." I illustrated on the blackboard. "Copy this, but don't worry if your forehead is higher or lower, your nose sharper, your chin more receding. Doesn't matter. It matters that you are trying to see, and reproduce, this line, trying to shut off the self-criticism, having a little adventure with this line."

"Now draw a line straight out from the top of the forehead, maybe half as long as the distance from forehead to neck. At the bottom of the neck line, draw a line parallel to the other one, a little longer. Then imagine an identical twin looking at the first face. At the open end of the lines, draw this identical twin facing the other face. Draw slowly—go out where the other line goes in, go in where the other one goes out. You get the idea. This is your right brain working, trying to see the lines, follow the lines."

I brought in a wax plant from the top of my bookcase in the office, asked a nearby student to hold it, and offered to draw it on the board without looking at the board. Every student watched, in silence, saw the leaves emerge, drape themselves down the blackboard, touch the chalk tray, cascade over each other sometimes. I set the plant on a chair in the middle of the room, asked them to slowly draw what they saw, without sneaking a look at their papers, without moving the papers.

Some went too fast, held their pencils too tightly, produced tight, hard loops. Others relaxed, captured the feel of the plant, the loose, easy flow of the leaves. One or two cheated, and looked, waited to see if I noticed. I noticed. We laughed. The differences in their drawings were obvious. It was their left/critical brain, telling them they were supposed to be perfect the first time. It was their jailer.

I asked them to notice that no two drawings were alike, date their drawings, see what happened in a few weeks, a few months, write a poem about the way it felt to do this drawing. Don't measure it. Don't find fault with it. Just notice what it felt like to do it.

Students walked around campus, the same campus they had walked on for a year, four years. They began to notice edges, saw the line the sky shared with a building, their backpack against the yellow concrete block wall, their friend's hair against the bulletin board. Edges appeared everywhere. They were there all the time. They just never noticed. Other details presented themselves: cobwebs in the restroom, ivy cracking the wall, snow piled on picnic tables, rows of caution lights at midnight in a deserted street. Writing became more visual, more specific, began to lose that generic sound.

THE MAN THING

A male student said in class that the main difference between men and women was that men could *spit*. Other males agreed, said women were not good spitters, hadn't mastered spitting, shouldn't spit. A male colleague told me he had an aunt who once spit from the observation deck of the tower at the University of Texas. He said his daughter practiced spitting to remain competitive with her male friends. One male student said spitting made men strong, macho, boss; women were not supposed to be strong, macho, boss. Women were supposed to be feminine, soft, gentle, supportive of spitting, as long as they themselves were not doing it.

The entire class insisted that male and female couldn't be the same, must be conditioned differently. They did not say why. They said they would raise their girls to play with Barbie dolls and their boys to spit. It was 1996. They were college students, getting a higher education than their friends who stayed home were getting.

Girls in 1996 still thought it was important to look cute, pretend to be helpless, and let their boyfriends change tires, paint the house, saw boards, and carry out the garbage. They themselves expected to fix meals, press the start button on the washer, burp babies, and brush toilet bowls with Clorox. Man and wife, not wife and man. They would find it silly to publish smiling photographs of men on the society page: John Smith engaged to Mary Brown. John Smith would be embarrassed to flash a diamond at his spitting friends. What would they think?

Mary could call John on the phone now, leave a message on his answering machine, say she called, but couldn't, wouldn't, ask John out, or pay the bill at the restaurant—unless, of course, she slipped her coins under the table. Tradition. What would her female friends think? They might expect her to spit! How vulgar—for a girl.

These girl mothers will teach their boys not to cry, not to express any feelings except anger, disgust, hostility, meanness, toughness, control, will cuddle their girl babies, look the other way when boy babies fall and bring their bleeding knees for kisses, will tell them to grow up and act like a man. They will have curfews for their girl babies, none for their boys, will expect their girl babies to be on the pill or be virgins, and their boy babies to gather sexual experiences as best they can. They will not think about it. They will not feel any responsibility for any of it, will not think about the tremendous power they have to create gentle, nurturing, warm men and strong, confident, able women. They will die not having thought about it. They will never get beyond spitting.

NINETY-NINE BOTTLES OF BEER IN THE ROAD

"Where there is no vision, the people perish."

Proverbs 29:18

Every morning, I walked my old miniature collie, Älska, along the country road in front of my house, a good twenty-five minutes from the nearest college town. I lived on the very top of a hill. Cars came up, passed in front of my property, and went down. I hardly ever saw them or heard them. But when Älska and I went walking, we found evidence that these cars had been there. In two weeks, this is what they left behind: two brown glass quart Genesee beer bottles with caps; one cardboard carton that once held six twelve-ounce bottles of Miller Lite (on the bottom of the carton, it said: "Keep America Beautiful/ Please Do Not Litter/ Please Recycle"); one clear plastic bottle, partially flattened, no label, white cap; two clear plastic twenty-ounce Coca-Cola bottles, one with a white cap; three blue and silver Busch Light cans; three red, blue, and silver Bud Light cans; two pint blue and silver Busch Beer cans, marked "World's Largest Recycler of Aluminum Cans"; one blue, gold, and brown Mug Cream Soda can; one pint blue, silver, and white Genny Light can; one clear glass Ocean Spray bottle; one paper wrapper from Long John Silver's; one twelve-ounce brown glass bottle without a label; two twelve-ounce brown glass Michelob Light bottles; two Marlboro Light packs; one yellow paper napkin, folded; five silver, white, and red pint Old Milwaukee cans; one twenty-ounce clear plastic Pepsi bottle; a brown glass quart beer bottle in a brown paper bag; one flattened Wild Cherry Pepsi can; and one can of Skoal Long Cut Wintergreen Smokeless Tobacco with "Packs Easy" and "Tastes Great" written on the top and "Warning: This Product Is Not a Safe Alternative to Cigarettes" written on the side.

Älska didn't know why this material concerned me, why I filled my arms with it two mornings in a row and took the car the third morning. She didn't realize that if thirty-two pieces of trash appeared in a space half a block long in two weeks, then we might expect over eight hundred pieces to appear there in a year.

Those who deposited their goods along the edge of my yard in this way must have been as indifferent about this as my dog—more so, in fact, since Älska at least sniffed and pawed at almost everything I collected.

Who could be using my property in this way? I didn't know. I doubted that it was Bill, the eighty-some-year-old farmer down the road, with the tiny well-groomed dog that yipped at my heels as I walked past on my five-mile route every morning. I doubted that my landlord had taken up any of these habits as his tractor bumped and clanked along my driveway on the way to his fields of corn and oats. It couldn't have been the family on the other side of the hill, taking a break from their nursery business to dump a little trash upwind from them. And I don't think my college students would have driven all this way every day to protest a low grade or two on their compositions and research papers. It was hard to picture all the local moms and pops heading out for a Sunday drive with all that beer in the car.

So though I hated to think so, it must have been mostly the teenage boys in our school district who knew of nothing better to do than drive around drinking and smoking and chewing and throwing their refuse out windows. It must have been their rite of passage—into—into *what*? Perhaps no dissertation had been written on this subject. But if one *were* written, it would, I think, be a dissertation about the illusion of freedom, and about whatever it was that made this illusion so attractive and so compelling.

College was not immune to it. For years, the local newspaper had been filled with stories about students' parties, fraternity initiations, rituals, about this excess and that. In town, the parties were all within walking distance of the school. In the country, the parties were smaller. They fit in a car, fit next to an old cemetery at the end of a dirt road, out by some abandoned barn. That was the main difference. I didn't live in town, didn't see what there was to see there at night, was not there when a few kids got together at a fraternity house for a couple beers, when someone dropped a cigarette on the sofa on the porch, started a small fire, put it out, went to bed, when the whole house burned down during the night, killing everyone sleeping there.

I was not there when one boy's mother crawled on her hands and knees in the ashes, looking for some trace, any trace, of her son that she lost so abruptly in the middle of his growing, did not see her find the book of Whitman's poems, the wrapper of quarters, the bits of smoked and jagged glass that were all that she had left of him, all that she had left except the pictures on the refrigerator, and an old sweatshirt, and memories piled on memories that all stopped at the age of twenty-three.

I know of these things because both the son and the mother were my students, and because she gave me the roll of quarters when, later, we built a garden in another painful place, when she said, "Here, Jimmy would want you to have these, would be glad to know that flowers came from them. And besides, I, too, have started a garden—for him, in memory of him. It is all, so far, I can think of to do."

I know that, over and over, she went back to the house, went alone mostly, went because it was the last place he was alive in, went because it gave her some solace, went because she had to go, because what else was there that she could have done? She knew that parents could not live their children's lives for them, could not know what was impossible to know, could not do what was impossible to do, could not ever get rid of what they did know, now, have crossed over a wide wilderness of grief that they cannot ever retreat from, have baptized themselves with grief in the name of the father and of the mother and of the son, and the brother, and the girlfriend, and of all the life that that son and his own children will never have.

These boys in the endless cars that crossed my quiet hilltop did not think of these things. And their parents, and teachers, and friends did not think of them either—until afterward.

NAMES

Fifty-five, mostly white, college students preparing to adopt fifty-five African American high school students in another city had just received a list of the names of the younger students. Many laughed condescendingly about the names, thought John and Mark and Bill and Frank and Heather and Erin were better names. They couldn't pronounce the new names, blamed the names.

I had not expected this, told them we would explore names tomorrow, asked them if they didn't know where their own name had come from to please call home and find out. The next day, I told them I had been named after my great-grandmother on the English side, whom we called Nan, whose name had really been Mary Clarinda, whose husband had been a carpet merchant, like his father before him, who had traveled around the world buying and selling carpets. It was his way of getting away from his Victorian wife, who did not know how to express affection for him, who, perhaps, had no affection to express. I told them they, nevertheless, had had one child, my grandmother, who, relatives said, Nan locked in a closet and left there while she went about her business elsewhere. I said I was sad to be named after such a woman and would change my name if I were not so used to it.

I told them my middle name was Swedish, was the same as my Swedish grandmother's middle name, and my mother's, told them this made up somewhat for my inheritance from the other side of the family. I said I had heard that my Swedish grandmother had allowed the doctor to choose a name for one of her daughters because she was so tired from having given birth that she couldn't be bothered with names.

I said my sister was named after a river, and I would have preferred that myself, would have been thrilled to be named after a river, depending on the river. I named my dog Älska, the root of the Swedish word *love*, and would have been happy to have been named Älska myself. I named my first dog Hede, after a character in a book by Selma Lagerlöf, a Swedish author, a man who had played the violin in his youth, as I had. I named my third dog after an emotionally abused child to demonstrate that if you raise something with love, it will grow strong, and happy, and healthy, will have bright, warm, mischievous eyes, will sit quietly next to you and watch the sun rise or set, will know how to play with anyone who loves animals, will know how to listen empathically, will be good at kissing.

I said it was the same with people. Our names meant something. Our names came from somewhere, provided us with continuity, history. The students shared their own stories, demonstrated that this was true for them too. I told them it was true for all people, told them to ask, check it out.

Students in the country thought the city was filled with homeless people. They didn't know any homeless people. We would soon be going to a city school to work with our adopted students. The college students were afraid they would run into homeless people, wanted to know what to think, what to do, what to say to them. All they knew so far was an image—maybe from television, maybe from a trip or two outside their home territory. I asked if they had talked to any homeless people in the last year or two or eighteen. No. They were scared of them. They were too aggressive, they always wanted money from you, they looked dirty, looked like they slept on cardboard. They would like to start a conversation, would like to give them money, but they might not be friendly, might not spend the money wisely.

We ordered subscriptions to *Real Change*, Seattle's homeless newspaper three thousand miles away, because *homeless* was such a stark stereotype to most non-homeless we knew and reminded us of other stereotypes, other fears. *Real Change* startled, encouraged, saddened, and, most of all, told one story at a time, brought us back to lives, brought us back to names. Everyone—one name, one life. Oh. They had not thought of it that way, but it was true. We collected names, lives, one week at a time—heard them, began to feel how it felt to have that name, live that life. I asked the college students how they felt about their upcoming visit to the city school. They told me they were afraid, afraid they would be shot, knifed, robbed, laughed at, called names, not liked, hated.

I asked them, afterward, what they learned from our first visit. They learned that it was not like that, not like that, not like that, not like that at all. Why did they ever think it would be? Why?

DRUGS

I know nothing about drugs, have a glass of wine once every two or three years on special occasions, rarely take medicine, walk five miles a day in good weather, eat well, prize my health and fitness.

My students knew a lot more about drugs than I did. Many of them thought of drugs as cool, called parties fun when their friends drank so much that they urinated on people's lawns or vomited or passed out or had sex with someone they hardly knew. They would have preferred that adults bless their entertainment of choice, consider it natural, and look the other way.

The school, and the local police, after many years of looking mostly the other way, cracked down now, busted noisy parties, busted large parties, aroused the ire and indignation of students. The school had half a dozen counselors in the guidance office to serve thousands. Some of the counselors had only master's degrees. Student Life personnel explained policies, enforced policies, informed students about responsible behavior. Some faculty listened to students who wanted to talk to them about their lives outside the classroom. Many did not, said it was none of their business, none of their interest, said they were not qualified to listen to such talk. "If they want to destroy their lives," some said, "that's their business. Who am I to question their decision?"

Mostly, students were on their own. The needs beneath the drinking and the drug use far too often went unmentioned, unexplored, and unmet. To a non-drinker like myself, these needs seemed complicated. Perhaps, to others, they were not. But sometimes I thought they went unmentioned and unmet because adults drank and used drugs for some of the same reasons the students did, and could not say so.

In one of my last semesters, I found myself with the angriest, most indifferent, most defiant class I had ever encountered. The class was a multicultural literature General Education course for students who were not English majors. It was a three-hour, three-credit small-group discussion course. Grades were to be based on a series of group projects that demonstrated the depth and breadth of students' understanding of the readings. They were free to plan almost any kind of project based on their selections from our readings for the course. They were free to compare/contrast—or in other ways connect—our readings with any literature they might wish to read outside the course assignments—or with stories, poems, and plays they might write themselves. I offered myself as a resource person—offered to bring questions for discussion if they needed them, to lead discussions if they were uncomfortable leading them, and to spend part of the class period in whole-class discussion of anything they might wish to explore in that way. Students understood these things at the beginning of the semester. No one dropped the course.

Usually, this approach worked well—worked better than whole-class discussion, got more students involved, brought out more interpretations, more responses. Almost always, students enthusiastically invented fresh ways of showing me how much thinking and discussing they had done. They tape-recorded themselves having discussions at home and asked me to listen to the tapes. They went to great, and often hilarious, trouble to videotape their versions of stories we read. They dramatized stories, built thematic units of poems, stories, and plays, synthesized various works, created interpretive dances and songs, did more than I myself would ever have thought of alone. They enjoyed themselves, entertained each other, took pride in what they did, challenged each other, competed with other groups to outdo each other—behaved professionally, knew their limits, knew their strengths.

This time was different. Oral presentations sometimes lasted only five minutes, group members sometimes did not appear at rehearsals, did not even appear in class when their presentations were scheduled. Some who did come invested nothing in their projects, did not explore the readings at all, had nothing to say but plot summaries, and sometimes ignored class assignments altogether and spent their time reading lyrics of popular songs aloud instead. They expected A's and B's for these presentations, and pouted, swore, slammed doors when they received lower grades, sometimes skipping class for weeks afterward.

I talked with them alone and as a whole class, tried to understand, tried to find out why they were investing so little in the course, tried to learn how we might change the course so that they could value it more. For weeks, no one would say anything—except that they didn't want to give up their small groups. Finally, after the worst group project, those responsible for it angrily announced that they had done poorly because they had never wanted to read multicultural literature in the first place. "Look at *me*," one of them said. "*I'm* not Chinese. Why should I read a Chinese story? *I'm* not Canadian. *I'm* not African. *I* don't speak Spanish. Why can't we read poems about white American teenagers? None of this other stuff is relevant!"

I reminded them that multiculturalism was what the class was *about*. I said it was helpful for me to know that they resented being asked to read the material for the class because, as I designed the course, this possibility had not occurred to me. I had thought they might feel the way I had felt as a student—so limited, and so unaware of so much of the world. I had designed the course this way because I didn't want them to be limited as I myself had been. And they were still free to read anything from anywhere and then use what they read to shed light on our literature. This light did not have to affirm any particular idea, or any particular literature. They were free to criticize anything, for any reason.

This was not enough. The entire class, they said, should have been devoted to stories, poems, and plays written by or about white American teenagers. I suggested that they might enroll in Creative Writing next year and experiment with writing their own stories or poems, but, other than that, I didn't know of any course where they might focus solely on writings by white American teenagers. After this conversation, one of the students wadded up her paper, threw it in the wastebasket, swore at me, and left the room.

When I went to my office after class, there was a message from her on my answering machine, apologizing. I called her back, told her I would like to write her a letter, but would not have time to do that for a few days. I offered to bring the letter to our next class. A few days later, I wrote the letter, discussed, at length, how much I wished to understand "where students were coming from" in our class, where *she* was "coming from." I said that I really did not want to end the semester with only the memories of her that I had gathered up to that point.

She was there, at the next class, accepted my letter but didn't read it until afterward, and participated in the class. The next week, she brought me a letter of her own in which she said that her mother was mentally ill, and in an institution, and it was her own responsibility to take care of the rest of the children in the family—to do everything a mother would do in her mother's absence—even though she was a college student at the same time and had to commute a long distance to class. She said her anger, really, was about having to live like that. It was about her mother's desertion of the family. It was not about me, and it had nothing at all to do with multicultural literature. It was just that she wanted to have a good grade point average, and, because she had so many responsibilities at home, she couldn't devote the time to her courses that they required. She didn't want to drop out of school, didn't want to take an incomplete grade, and didn't know what to do.

At about this time, one group of students asked if they could do their class presentation on drug lyrics. I told them yes, provided they "do something" with the literature we had been reading as well. They did a survey of the class, asked if class members had ever taken drugs, which drugs they had taken, which of the lyrics they were already familiar with, and when they were most likely to listen to them. They told me they believed that most students knew these lyrics well, listened to this music when they were high, were high as often as they themselves were, and used drugs for the same reasons. They wanted me to know, they said. They knew I didn't know.

Thirty out of thirty responded to their survey. Almost all of them said that they had used drugs; almost all of them said they used them regularly, used them several times a week. What did these lyrics say to them when they were *not* high? They said, "These are the groups who use drugs; these are people who live and feel the way I live and feel." Just knowing that, they said, made them feel as if they were part of a community, made them feel as if they belonged somewhere.

"Without them," I asked, incredulously, "You feel as if there is no place where you belong?"

"*Yes,*" they said. "Yes. Absolutely. All the time." They didn't belong in the academic part of school, didn't belong in their majors, didn't belong at home. Their families didn't know them. The chance of getting a good job with their grades was slim; it was pretty much impossible. They had no idea where to go after they left here. They had no idea whether they would graduate or not. They didn't know how to pull up their grades at this late date. They couldn't afford to start over somewhere else. And there was nobody who gave a damn. And that was why they wished the course could be about *them*, because it was their only chance to have some hope that things could be better, to have some hope that they could find a path out of this mess that was their lives, the only lives they had, the only lives they would ever have.

This presentation came near the end of the semester. I told colleagues about it. I told administrators. Some said, "I'm not surprised." Some said it made them sad to hear it. No one said, "We need to deal with this." No one.

I didn't know how to deal with it. How did one deal with a class full of orphans, a class full of people who had made such serious mistakes by the age of twenty or twenty-one that they didn't know how to un-make them? Were they the only students on campus who felt this way? Were there thirty more? Three hundred more? Three thousand more? More? Where did they come from? What did they do in high school? Why had their parents washed their hands of them? How could there be so many homes without homemakers, so many communities with no sense of community?

"I can't go up to a guy and tell him I'm interested in him without being drunk," a girl said. "If I'm not drunk or high, people are boring. If I'm not drunk or high, I feel completely alone."

This is what it meant when they said multicultural literature wasn't relevant. It meant, "My tolerance for pain is used up." It meant, "I'm okay if I just don't think, if I just don't feel anything. But if I think about anyone's life, I think about *my* life, and from here, where I am, my life looks like it hasn't gone anywhere yet, and it's not going anywhere in the future either—not anywhere that anybody would want to go."

CHAPTER 4

"Nada Y Pues Nada":
The Kids Nobody Wanted

"NADA Y PUES NADA"

"Some lived in it and never felt it but . . . it all was *nada y pues nada y nada y pues nada.*"

Ernest Hemingway, "A Clean, Well-Lighted Place"

I had just finished ten years listening to the same group of gifted students I had started with in third grade. I saw, week by week and year by year, how they lost their enthusiasm for learning, how they resigned themselves to doing whatever they decided they had to do to earn the grades their parents expected them to earn, to please whatever teachers they had decided needed pleasing. I saw how boring so many of their classes were, how bossy and condescending and unimaginative so many of their teachers were, how repetitious their days and years were. And I heard, week by week and year by year, how much they resented it all.

I was curious to learn what attitudes and circumstances I would find if I started with a new group of ninth graders, students I had not known in their younger years, students who were not necessarily labeled gifted, and asked the high school principal what he thought of that. There were many ninth graders whom teachers "couldn't stand," he said, and I would be welcome to work with them.

What teachers didn't like was their attitude. They were "nothing like" those in my first group, who had just graduated. "Your kids," he said, "turned out different from the others. I don't know what you did exactly, but you had some kind of cumulative effect on them."

What he meant was that they hardly ever caused trouble, they were the leaders of the school, and they were eager to try new things. Many were outstanding athletes. Several excelled in more than one sport. But they were also outstanding academically. A number were Eagle Scouts. Every year, these same students tried out for the school musical, and some played leading roles, in spite of the fact that they had never sung or danced in public in their lives. They had a sense of humor. They were resilient. They were a pleasure to be around. They got things done. They thought about other people's needs, and not just their own.

The new ninth graders were not like this. They were passive, critical, unenthusiastic, limp by comparison. Why? The principal didn't know. The teachers I talked to didn't know either. Some just said that students "came in groups" like that. One year, you'd have a great bunch of kids; the next year you would have the opposite.

So that September, I was expecting the worst: sullen, uncooperative, bad-tempered, nasty kids, whom no one could stand, and who would thoroughly challenge my faith in the nature, and potential, of children. I walked into the ninth grade English class, introduced myself, told the students a few stories about how my college students and students in the ten-year project felt about school, and said I very much wanted to know how they felt too. I said that someday, after they had become adults, I wanted to write a book about these things, and I wanted their thoughts and feelings to be in the book, but, mostly, if they were un- happy, I wanted them to feel better, and if they were happy, I wanted to help them stay that way. I said my project was voluntary, and if they decided they didn't want to participate in it, they didn't have to, but I hoped they would stay with me until they graduated.

In terms of attitude, I saw no difference between these students and those in the ten-year project. They had the same kinds of stories to tell about their lives and about their years in school. They experienced the same kinds of pain and welcomed the same kinds of encouragement and understanding. If the principal had not warned me, I would never have known that these students were the same ones their teachers had accused of being hostile and uncooperative. To me, they could not have been more eager and enthusiastic and open, and they welcomed me into their lives as much as I welcomed them into mine.

At first, I was astounded by this and wondered if I was just seeing what I wanted to see. I looked for differences, waited for them to appear, but they never did. After a few months with them, I began to call guidance counselors at large and small, urban and rural schools within a day's driving distance of my home, and asked for permission to work with a total of about one hundred ninth graders who were unhappy, including some teachers didn't like, some who were failing, who abused drugs and alcohol, who came from unhappy homes, who had criminal records, who were often in in-school and out-of-school suspension. I said I could probably handle about a hundred. The first seven schools I called eagerly welcomed me. Every school, they said, had far more than one hundred students like those I had described.

In between my college classes, I traveled to at least one school each week, often to two or three. One school had arranged for an entire gym full of students to meet with me, but the guidance counselor had told them nothing at all about me, or about why I was there. There was no microphone. Students sat on huge step risers on one side of the room. The guidance counselor and I stood at the bottom.

"This is Dr. Gill," she said, and walked out.

"Did the guidance counselor explain to you why I'm here?" I asked.

"No!" those in the front rows answered.

"Okay, then," I said. "This is it. I teach in a college where college students are not confident in their minds, where, many times, no one seemed to have listened to them before. I figured they learned this lack of confidence in their schools, and in their homes, and in their communities. I am here because I think you know how this happened, and, if you do, you will be a big help to all of us."

All the students in the auditorium became totally quiet. I went on: "I was expecting to meet with a few students at a time, so all I have is this little tape recorder, a tablet, and a pencil. What I would like to do is pass the tape recorder around to people who feel a little shy about talking in such a large group. Please speak clearly and slowly into it for about five minutes, and then pass it on to someone else. I would like you to give your name, but if you don't want to, that's all right. The rest of us will talk. Please be sure that I can hear you."

This huge group talked patiently, clearly, one at a time, for an entire class period. They talked about how boring their teachers were, how it took them a class period just to hand papers back or to take attendance. They talked about how lonely they were. They talked about how afraid they were that they would get into drugs, like so many of their friends already had. They talked about how hard it was to communicate with their families. They talked about how much racism there was in the town and how hard it was to get a job.

At another school, at least a hundred angry students were sent to a cafeteria, where I was expected to address them, again with no microphone and no explanation about why they were chosen and why I was there. I asked them to sit with their friends. I said I wanted to ask them the same question I asked my college students at the beginning of a semester: "Is school pain or pleasure for you?" I took notes on their answers, and collected their names, addresses, and phone numbers on note cards. For the next four years, I met with these students, almost always in these same groups.

At another school, I was given everyone who was in in-school suspension on the day I first arrived. Some of them were juniors and seniors. All they were told was that a college professor wanted to talk to them, and they had about twenty minutes. Several conference tables were arranged in a large square that filled the room. Sixteen of us sat around the table, four on a side. I explained why I was there. We went around the table and introduced ourselves by sharing one experience that affected how we felt at that moment. Every student told about a time when he or she had felt hurt, frightened, or angry. One of the older students began to talk about what it was like to be locked up in jail. All sixteen of us leaned forward in our seats, absorbed thoroughly in what he said. He talked for two hours. The guidance counselor told me afterward that she had tiptoed to the door many times, intending to send the students back to class, but when she saw that we were so totally engaged, she decided not to disturb us.

In another school, I was given four girls and four boys. I met separately with the girls and the boys. All of them were angry about the way they were treated in school, but the girls were by far the angriest. Some were planning to move to another school. Some were planning to drop out. In a few months, all the girls had left school. One of the boys had been suspended for calling a teacher a name as he passed him in the hall. He was a very lively, funny, spontaneous, impulsive boy. It was easy to imagine him saying what he said. For most of the first year, I asked him to meet with me individually so he could do all the talking. Eventually, all four boys met with me together.

In another school, I met with a room full of students who were planning to drop out. All of them were bitter and angry about their lives and believed that school was doing them no good. Within months, all but one of them had dropped out. I visited classes of the only remaining student so that I could see how teachers treated him, and so I could ask the teachers for their help in encouraging this boy to remain in school, to feel wanted, respected, and welcome, but none of his teachers liked him. One laughed when I told him that this boy was very sad and lonely. He said the boy slept in class almost every day. He assumed he was out drinking every night.

He never asked him why he slept, and never woke him, so he never found out, until I told him, that he had only one friend, an elderly carpenter he admired, and, this year, his friend had been diagnosed with terminal cancer. The boy went to the hospital regularly to visit him, but now the man was delirious and no longer knew who he was. He also had a job, which required him to work long hours, and he came from an abusive home. The teacher was not at all touched by this story and laughed even as I told it. He told me there were a lot of students like that. They were all just lazy and irresponsible and not worth the trouble it took to care about them.

The guidance counselor recommended that this student quit school and get a GED, even though there was no way he could continue to work and also attend GED classes. I met with him, in his home, for the rest of the year.

In the next three years, I drove 93,000 miles to meet with the rest of the students in these groups. Although they were almost all miserable and filled with anger about their schools and their lives, every one of them treated me with absolute respect, and almost all of them graduated. Some of those who did not wrote or called to tell me they had earned their GED.

These students, at every school, followed a very clear pattern, which is worth noting. In the first year, they met with me regularly, apologizing and sending word when they were absent or when they had to miss our session for another reason. I sent a newsletter to all of them, which their parents also sometimes read. Some students, and some parents, wrote to me. All the students were proud to be part of this group, and felt "special" because of it. Some said it was the first time they had ever been singled out for positive attention; usually, they went to the office because they were in some kind of trouble. Never once did any of them do anything in our group to jeopardize their special status as group members.

In that first year, hardly any of these students called me by name. They came to our sessions and spoke angrily about whatever angered them until it was time for them to go back to class. I listened, I sympathized, I asked for clarification, and I did my best to empathize. Their lives were difficult and painful, and I was very aware that, at the end of our sessions, they would return to their difficult and painful lives, and I would drive home to my life, which was almost idyllic compared with theirs.

From the first day of their second year with me, every student, at every school, called me by name, though I had never requested it, and, in fact, never mentioned it. Throughout the second year, they continued to tell me stories about their lives, all of them filled with anger, and hurt, and sadness, and disappointment.

At the beginning of their third year with me, students began to "dress up." Boys came with shorter, cleaner hair, and clean, wrinkle-free, new-looking shirts. Girls styled their hair, changed their makeup, wore unique, colorful clothes, intended their clothes to be a statement about themselves.

By the beginning of their fourth year, everyone was studying and trying to pass. Some of them, who spent part of each day at a vocational-technical (vo-tech) school, invited me to come with them to watch them at their work and to meet their teachers. They were proud of their teachers there and wanted to do a good job for them. Their teachers there cared, they said, and treated them respectfully, as adults. They thrived on this kind of treatment.

Even in their fourth year, all the students still had a great deal of anger to express, but now many of them also had the energy to go beyond complaining, to analyze, to explore ideas, to connect ideas with their lives, to imagine a life that was different, and better, than the one they had, to take some steps to approach that kind of life. Some, however, still lived precariously, ambivalently, on the edge between hope and despair, tired, beaten down, afraid to imagine something better, afraid to believe, to give themselves permission, to give themselves encouragement, to have the life they wanted.

After each visit, I left these schools filled to capacity with the tremendous, cumulative pain of "my kids'" lives. Sometimes I left with throbbing headaches. In the fourth year, after deciding that meeting parents might help cure my headaches, I visited the families of several of the unhappiest students.

I felt the tension and anger in those homes. I saw how family members talked to each other and how they sat in silence. I listened to what they talked about and contrasted it with what we talked about in our sessions. I saw some of the things they valued, and didn't value. I saw how invisible the teenagers were, and had been, how little real dialogue went on in their lives, felt how it must have felt to have no empathy, no affirmation, and no encouragement—ever.

I knew that, at the end of these four years, I would not have solved *any* of the huge problems that these young people had to face if they were to go on with their lives, if they were to improve their lives. I knew that four years is not very long when so many more years have been filled with grief, and intense loneliness, and little else. I knew that if they were to succeed in healing themselves, they would have to reparent and reteach themselves, would have to discover how to give themselves the guidance, the encouragement, and the raw hope that their parents and their schools had never given them, would have to feel both entitled to that guidance, encouragement, and hope, and responsible for seeking out ways to provide it. I knew this would not be easy, and I knew that, sometimes, they would believe it was impossible. But I also knew that all of us, in our groups that had continued to meet throughout these years, had taken steps to create at least an understanding of what sustained acceptance, positive attention, empathy, and dialogue could do, and I hoped that would be enough.

SCREW 'EM ALL

"You know what their problem is?" he said. "Their whole life they've been choosing things for me. Like, 'We usually buy *these* clothes.' It's *my* money. I buy what I want. They'll say, 'How about a *green* pair of pants?' I'm not buyin' them. They'll get all offended. It's my money, and they can't *do* nothin'."

His parents were saying they'd like more control over him. They wished he weren't getting old enough to be beyond their control. They wished he were different, wished he were more like them. He didn't know why they behaved this way. And then, to make matters worse, they said, "All right, then," and they bought something nice for his younger brother and got him nothing. "See how he feels *now!*"

their actions said. There was more than one way to let him know they were still in control. They did this until they were so polarized that all he could say without selling his soul was "No."

His parents were divorced before he was a year old. He thought his father was a jerk. When he saw him walking down the street, he looked the other way. It didn't happen often. His father lived in another state, ten hours away. Last time he saw him, he was eight. Eight. He was seventeen now. So it was his grandmother who took charge, who helped everyone, helped his uncle, his father, his brother, helped everyone but him, helped them because she approved of what they were spending the money on. He wanted a car, a '72 car. It would cost twelve hundred dollars. They'd contribute ten thousand dollars for this little "hunk o' crap" four years old. They wouldn't listen to him, wouldn't trust his judgment about cars, told him they didn't want to talk about it, told him that was final. He just wanted a *loan*. He wasn't asking them to *buy* it. Just a *loan*. Nothing doing. Forget about it. Leave them alone.

I called his mother and asked if I could meet her at her workplace. She agreed. I walked in. She greeted me. The first thing she said was that she hated both of her sons, thought they were both despicable. They never spoke to each other. The sons walked in; she walked out. They didn't eat meals together. If she took them somewhere in the car, they drove in total silence.

Something occurred to me. "By any chance does your son remind you of your ex-husband?"

"Spittin' image," she said. "Spittin' image."

She told me how hard it had been, raising boys. Ever since he was small. She remembered Christmas, when he was four or so. He didn't get what he wanted, threw a temper tantrum, started screaming, wouldn't stop. She went after him, up the stairs. She beat him and beat him and beat him while he was trying to pull away, trying to get up the stairs. "This'll teach you," she said. "This'll teach you."

It didn't teach him. It just made him bitter, just made him feel more and more deprived and alone.

YOU LIVE UNDER MY ROOF

"I'm doin' very well," she said. "It could be better. I got B's, C's, and I got an A—which I shouldn't have got. But I could have done better."

It was the teacher, she said. But she was doin' good. She struggled. But, you know, she went to work and everything. She worked at the hospital. She went to school five days a week and worked six days, four hours each day, sometimes eight on the weekends. She worked both Saturday and Sunday, had Tuesdays off. That was a long time. She did it because it was good experience, and because she wanted to do a lot of things she needed money for. She couldn't be depending on her parents all the time. Besides, she was going to be moving in with her dad soon, would be staying with him until she joined the Marines.

Her mom was going to be moving too, but she would be eighteen by then, so she would have a choice about which parent to live with. She would choose her father, because she and her father were real close. He understood her. She could say anything in front of him, could sit down and talk to him. He didn't say, "Well, you live under my roof and you gotta do this, and you gotta do that." Her mom was strict. Her mom was very strict. Her dad was not strict. Her dad understood that a child was a child, that a child had to do things, had to grow up. She *was* growing up. She made up her own mind. She was not easily influenced. She had willpower, could say no in a minute.

She liked to go out, was an outgoing person, loved to do things. Her mom was like, "You can't go here, and you can't go there." Sometimes she went anyway and suffered the consequences when she got home. She told her dad what she did and everything. Her dad knew where she was coming from. Her mom was just too strict. In middle school, eighth grade, she had had to come in when it got dark. She had been like, "Mom! Come *on!* It's dark at six or seven or eight." Her mom had raised her since she was six or seven, but her dad had raised her too. They had just never lived together. Her dad told her to be in at a certain time. She gave him a phone number, told him where she would be. She really would be there.

Her mom had been through a lot and was trying to protect her. Her mom would say, "Be in at ten or eleven." She would be like, "But Mom! The party doesn't start until nine!" So she'd stay out longer and be grounded for two weeks. Once she was grounded for a month. She used to sneak out. It was terrible.

It was better now. Her mom didn't worry so much, really. It wasn't so hard, if you let 'em know where you were. But if she told her mom she was goin' over to a guy's house, her mom would kill her. They usually said the father was overprotective, but, you know, in her case, it was her mom. Sometimes she acted too young, and sometimes she acted too old. It was hard to act your age all the time.

Maybe she thought too much. She thought of all the possibilities ahead of time, tried to think about the negatives too, because you never know. What if this happened? What if that happened? How would she react? You try to think what's the worst thing that could happen so you can prepare yourself.

Sometimes she got angry, took it out on her friends, took it out on somebody—because you can't hold it in. You can't hold it all in. The more you talk about it, the more it helps. She could tell her dad anything. He just wanted to sit back and watch her and see if she did it right. She wouldn't always do it right. When she was having problems with her boyfriend, she acted ignorant sometimes. She tried to act like she didn't care. But deep down inside, it bothered her. It hurt her, what her boyfriend was doing, but she didn't tell him that. She would feel too helpless. If she kept tellin' him, it wasn't going to do anything, so sometimes she had to wait a while, had to struggle. Because if it was too easy, he would think he could get anything he wanted. So she held back, but not too much, not so much that he would pull away and leave her.

HE JUST GOT COMPLETELY LOST

Science class wasn't that boring, he said. Reading class wasn't that boring. The boring ones were French and math—and study hall, because there was nothing to do in there. In French, he didn't know what they were *saying*. He *used* to do his homework. He just got completely lost. He didn't have any idea what was going on.

He was taking French because he wanted to go to college. You have to take two years of a language to go to college, so he was taking French. But he was failing it, failing it with a zero percent. He just went in there and fell asleep. It was first-year French, and he was lost from the beginning. He couldn't remember nothing. He didn't know any words in French. Some teachers, if you don't understand something, they go back, but that's very few teachers. It was because they didn't care. They just came, did what they were paid to do. That was all. They had two exchange students at their house. That was pretty interesting, but they were his sister's friends. They weren't there now.

He wanted to go to college to play football. He liked football better than basketball, better than any sport. It was more physical. Basketball got pretty physical, but not as physical as football. Forward and center were under the basket the whole time. He'd been playing football for nine years. His father played football too, would have been in the majors, except that he hurt his knee. He himself hurt his ankle a couple weeks ago. It hurt pretty bad. He sprained it playing basketball, landed on it like this. It was all swollen. He couldn't walk right. Their next game was Saturday. Their team hadn't lost a game yet. He sure would like to be able to play.

Well, anyway, he needed the French to go to college, needed two years. The teacher was going to talk to a counselor about it. As of the first of March, she hadn't done anything about it. He couldn't go to the counselor himself. It would be too much of a hassle. You had to fill out papers and everything, and find some other course to take, like a shop class. He would like a shop class, actually. It was just that he would feel funny coming down and saying he was failing French. If you're failing something, it's like you're a failure yourself.

His sister took French, took French and German both. She tried to teach him. She taught him better than the teacher. The teacher went too fast. She talked French the whole time. He didn't know what she said. That was why he got lost, you know? She said everything in French, and he had no idea what she was saying.

SO THERE WERE FIFTEEN OF US IN THE BACK OF THIS TRUCK

"There was more went than planned," she said, "Because they didn't have rides to go down, so they had to pick up all these people. And there was fifteen of us in the back, there was three in the front, and then the car behind us was seven or eight. So we got down there, and we had like six cases of beer, and everybody hopped in the back of the truck. There was maybe twenty-six people in the back of this truck. It was really crowded, and we were drinkin,' and we seen this flashlight shinin' through the back of the cab, and I'm like, 'Shit!'"

So the cops asked if there was anybody over twenty-one there, and there was only one, so he got to go free. He wanted to know who owned the truck and everything, and the girl next to her almost said his name, but she told the girl not to, because he was on probation and everything.

"Just be quiet," she told her. So nobody said anything, and the guy that was driving told the officer just to take whatever beer was left and let them go. There were only four or five beers left. And that's what he did. He let them go. They would have had to pay a five-hundred-dollar fine—each. The guy that thought of that, he was a really smart person. The police told them to pile out of the truck one at a time so they could check their eyes and see how they were walking, and then they just let them go, except for one guy that got caught with, like, cocaine, and pot. But he was in the other car. He got caught, and got a thousand-dollar fine.

That was all before the concert even started. They were just in the parking lot. So they went in, and the concert was fantastic. When this one song came on that's on MTV all the time, that used to be number one on the countdown, there was like, helicopters and lights flashing everywhere, and everybody, the whole stadium, was singing it. It was so great. It was really fun.

So the concert was great, and after the concert they told everybody to meet back at the truck, but everybody was going down on the floor, and they were throwing people up in the air and everything, and this one guy came running up and saying that he had backstage passes, but by then she was out by the truck, so they had to wait out there for a long time. The concert ended around eleven-thirty or twelve—on a school night. She told her mom she didn't know what time she would be home. So the rest of them came out around two-thirty in the morning, and they were standing there, drinking and doing nothing the whole time, because they didn't have the keys to the truck. They were freezing to death. So the rest of them came back about two-thirty. They got autographs and everything. They were so happy. She finally got home about three-fifteen. It was terrible getting up the next morning. She didn't have a hangover or anything. She was just so tired. But she went to school.

It wasn't hard getting served. Everybody always thought she was older. And besides, they always went to the same place, so they knew them, and they didn't think anything of it. Her mom never said anything about it. Her mom trusted her. Her mom knew she knew what she was doing.

UP AGAINST THE WALL

They were in tenth grade or eleventh grade. It depended on how many times they had to repeat a grade. This one guy was looking at the third time in tenth grade because he wouldn't suit up for gym, he wouldn't wear those bluish shorts and that white shirt. He wouldn't run around the gym and shoot baskets and all that, and he wouldn't take swimming, so they flunked him, but nothing changed. He wouldn't suit up the next year either.

So we were talking about how school used to be, and how, if you went back far enough, like to first grade, or second, or third, or whatever, it was okay, because at least you got to be there with your friends. But really it wasn't okay then either, because there wasn't ever a time when they weren't getting in trouble for something. Like in kindergarten, this chick was up on the monkey bars, and him and his friend walked up, and she started to cry. The teacher came up, grabbed him by the hood and all, and put him up against the wall for like, a week. This wall, it went down into the basement or something like that. And whenever people were bad, they lined up against the wall, and you just had to stand there and watch all the other people play. In a whole year, he must've had recess five times. That's all. All the time he was against that wall. Man!

School was great, in the old days—kindergarten, first grade, second, third, fourth. He didn't *like* school, but it was fun to be there. It was a ball—chasing girls and all. He beat up a girl once, a strong girl. She was always looking for a fight, you know? This guy got in a fight with some kid, and he threw the milk on her. He threw the milk on her, and she threw it back. She just started going off on everybody. Every time they went out for recess, she was like, being in a fight with someone. They used to play kickball. She started yelling at everyone, and everyone was telling her to calm down, so he got in there, and he was like, "Calm down! Calm down!" And she was spitting and everything, and she smacked him.

And this other guy, he went to a private school. He was the first one to get suspended from that school. That was fourth grade. That was a pretty good school too. A kid threw a piece of slate at him, and he had to have stitches. Him and his friends beat him up the next day. Once, in kindergarten, he gave a girl the finger. The teacher paddled his *ass*. It was a *zoo* in that class. She grabbed him, and she was like shaking him, and yelling at him, "Shut up! Shut up!"

There was this one teacher, she crunched his brother's knuckles with a ruler. And this other time, him and this guy were playing ball—it was like, first grade, and he had like, kicked the ball in his face, and he didn't mean to do it, so he was looking at his face to see if he was okay and all, but the teacher thought he was beating up on him, so she took him to the bathroom and got about ten rulers with the band around them and whapped his ass about three times. Ten rulers! She wrapped them together with a rubber band around them. And his mom wouldn't believe him. "A teacher wouldn't *do* that!" she said. Three times! She kicked his ass *good*! His dad wouldn't believe him either. But then his dad did believe him, and they were gonna get the lady fired, but they found out she couldn't be fired because she had taught there too long. Go figure.

TRUE LOVE

This is how it was. It was true love, and you didn't even know it. Say she was going out with John. And they'd been going out for two years. And the whole time, she always thought this guy Dan was good-looking and all, but she was going out with John. No doubt about it. She had all these feelings and all. But then John moved up to Connecticut or some shit, and she was with this guy, and she was constantly telling Dan her problems with this guy. And the next thing you know, they were kissing good-bye every once in a while. Then she was sitting back, and Dan asked her to the prom, and they were going out, and she was thinking, "I can't believe we're going out!" So they were going out for a while, and then they were always doing things together, and she sat back and she thought. She couldn't think straight, you know. She couldn't even pass school, cuz this dude was always on her mind. She couldn't work, she got fired, because she couldn't do the job, because she was always thinking about this guy. She was a waitress, and she was writing this stuff on a pad: Dan, Dan, Dan.

The love she had with John was a total love. It was friendship, it was loyalty, it was sex. But the love she had for Dan was just a friendship, a brotherly kind of love, because he was always there for her. But he wasn't a real, big, *true* love. So there were all these different kinds of love. They were all love.

And there was self-love, too. You should always love yourself. She hated herself. Seriously. She was so down on herself. Sometimes she completely and totally hated herself. So she got depressed. If you had too much self-love, you had conceit. But if you had too little, you had depression. That was the way it was.

There were all these different kinds of love. One person loved his car and money, and another one loved this girl because of her house and the food in the refrigerator. Say there were Chuck A and Chuck B. Chuck A had good looks and a great personality and a piece of shit car. He was nice, and he treated you real good. But he had no money. And then there was Chuck B, an asshole who always only thought of himself and who had a lot of money, but who beat you all the time. Which one should she choose? She should choose the one that treated her the best.

This was how it was with the car. The other guys, they didn't know you. They went to their class every day. It was like, "How you doin'?" Then they found out you had a Porsche. A Corvette. Yeah, a Porsche. Then it was, "What's *up*? How ya *doin'*? Oh, my *God*! You look so *good* anymore!" That was materialistic love. That was how the world was. You couldn't trust anybody.

This is weird, but you could look at it this way too. If you had something, you could show love for it and take care of it. There are things and people we love, but we can't show that we love them because we don't have them to take care of yet. So this is going to sound a bit stupid. You could love helicopters. All your life, you always wanted to go get a pilot's license. You didn't even have a driver's license yet, but you wanted a pilot's license. That's the point. You love helicopters. But you don't have one yet. You love the design. You love the concept.

The trouble is, the world is falling apart. It's one big pile of shit! It's awful. But it's all cuz of *us*, though. It's inside of us—the good and the bad. This is society today. You gotta have a nice car. You gotta have a job. You gotta have the money. You gotta have the girls. You gotta have the guys. You gotta have everything, like, to go somewhere.

So how do you get it? That's the question. We're all headed in the same direction. There's the top of the mountain. We're each taking a different trail. Who knows if the trails are all equal or not? You don't know that till you get there. And then, you know, it might be too late. It would be good if you could know—is my path okay or not? But you don't know.

THEY SHOULD TREAT YOU LIKE A *PERSON*, INSTEAD OF A *STUDENT*, YOU KNOW?

It was never like this, before the new superintendent came. I mean, there were good teachers and bad teachers, but some of them had respect, you know? But now there's nothing. There's nobody that listens to you, really. They just talk. They talk and talk. And if you don't get it, that's too bad. I mean, what else can you do?

You get put in in-school suspension for six days for using vulgar language, and you didn't. So you don't go one day, and so they give you twelve days. You can't do nothing about it. They give you a slip, and it has your name on it, and so you have to go. If your parents come to school to defend you, it will be worse, because, first of all, your father has a temper, and second of all, the teacher would take it out on you afterward. So you take it out on yourself. You tell them, "Okay. I didn't do nothing. So now I will. Now I will be bad, and then I will deserve what you do," and they're like, "So go ahead." They don't care. There is nothing else you can do, because you're just kids.

The guidance counselor, he says, "Just come in anytime you have a problem. That's what we're here for" and all that, but when you go in there, he doesn't do nothing. You've been in there plenty of times, and he just brushes you off. They don't listen. They tell you that stuff because they just want to get you off their back. They fired the only nice teacher. The parents all complained and everything, but it didn't do any good. Because she was different. She liked kids. She understood kids. So they got rid of her. They laugh at you, or they pat you on the back and say, "We're sorry. We can't help you."

You just have to do what they say. You do better if you like the class. You do worse if you don't like it. It depends on the teacher a lot. If the teacher treats you like they're supposed to, then everybody's okay. But if they don't, then nobody does good at all. They should treat you like a person instead of a student, you know? Treat you as if they've known you, and they understand what you're trying to do, and know that you're trying—that you're trying to pass their class. They should notice that you're trying. And a lot of the teachers don't. If you don't do good, they scream and holler. They won't even let you try. They just say, "Aw, *you* can't do it!"

So you're really unhappy here. You like the kids, most of the kids, but not the way the teachers are. They yell at you and stuff. If you try to do something and it doesn't work out, they just sit there and scream in your face, and it's like, "Shut up! I don't know how to do it! Leave me alone!" They really do scream. And you can't do nothing about it. If you sit there and try to do something, and somebody's screaming in your face, what are you supposed to do? You tried!

What else can you do? The only thing to do is scream back, so you scream back. It's like when you get in a fight with your mother. You just scream back. That way you let things out. It's better than hitting everybody! You'd *like* to hit them! That's what a lot of them *need*! You've come close sometimes.

Teachers, they like their power. That's the truth. They enjoy it. It's like when you were little. Adults know they can get away with it, so they do it. As long as they can get away with it, they yell. Because how many schools do you know that's going to take the kid's word over the teacher's?

WHO WANTS TO SIT IN A SUB SHOP ON FRIDAY NIGHT?

Last night I went to a film about hiking the Brooks Range in Alaska. They're taking a group of college students this summer. Part of the film shows them hiking up to the top of Mt. McKinley. It showed the leader standing at the very top. When they were hiking over the Brooks Range, they met an Eskimo on a snowmobile. They never saw a person anywhere, and all of a sudden here was this snowmobile with a gun sticking out of it. They took a picture of it.

The director asked why he was there, and he said, "*No*! Why are *you* here?"

He said he'd been setting traps and was going around and collecting whatever he found there. The director asked him what he would do if the snowmobile broke down, and he said, "I *fix*!" I guess so! Two hundred miles from home, with nothing but snow and ice in every direction!

Well, let's talk about school. How are your classes going?

"They all suck."

"Really? Not a single good class? Not even study hall? Last time I was here, you said you liked accounting because at least you learned something practical there. Well, how many classes do you have ulcers over?"

"*All* of them!"

"English isn't too bad. You can write about whatever you want to. I wrote about Michael Jordan. He's *amazing*! He's six-six, he's twenty-two years old, plays for the Chicago Bulls—averages about thirty points a game. He earns three million *dollars*!"

"That would be *nice*, huh? . . . I'll tell you something that bothers me a lot. At one school I used to visit, everyone in my group dropped out—except one girl, and now she's dropped out too. I never got to know her well. She does LSD, and she does cocaine. She's a pretty girl. She's a talented girl. She has a lot of things going for her, but—she's really messed up her life. I go to another school where everybody I talk to—except one girl—is on drugs. That girl is graduating this year. Why do people *do* so much of that?"

"It's more fun when it's not legal."

"I see that a lot of people feel that way. It takes ingenuity to get it—and get yourself home afterward."

"Who wants to sit in a sub shop on Friday night?"

"What else is there to do?"

"You can sit at the sub shop."

"You can ride around."

"You can wait for your parents to leave."

"You can fool around."

"You can get drunk."

"It's pretty much fun watchin' somebody else get drunk an' passin' out."

"At the last school I went to, we talked about the meaning of life."

"You get up, go to school, and play sports. Every day! The same thing, *every day*!"

"You can get a job."

"What?"

"Get a job."

"That's all?"

"What else *is* there?"

KINDERGARTEN WAS THE WORST

"If I asked you to think back to a time when school was a pleasure, how far back would you have to go? Kindergarten?"

"Kindergarten was the worst!"

"Really!"

"Drove me insane."

"Me too."

"Yeah. They used to lock a shelf down on top of a kid."

"Once I let a big dog out the window."

"She had a big paddle. She'd hit you, and you would just smile and walk away."

"Did you have any male teachers in elementary school?"

"One—third grade. He was cool."

"So when you're parents, what will you do with your kids?"

"I'm not going to have any kids. I don't even want to *know* about kids."

"Would you let them get paddled in school?"

"Sure."

"It's like a fraternity initiation or something? I had to go through it, so you have to go through it too?"

"*Yeah!*"

"What good would it do? Why do it, if it doesn't do any good?"

"Memories."

"Even if it did do some good, maybe there's a better way. Some people never get hit by anyone in their whole lives! Maybe that would be a different kind of experience! . . . So what do parents use, instead of hitting?"

"My mom yells."

"Does it work?"

"No. She yells. It's *funny*, to hear people yell. She *always* yells."

"I ask a simple question, and get a smart-mouth answer, so I start yellin' at her. She started yellin' and screamin', and I go, '*Mom!*' She hit my car! Out in the street!"

"She hit your *car?*"

"She hit my car. She won't hit it again!"

"My mom, she said, 'I'm goin' to take your car keys away from you.' I told her I'd slit her *tires!*"

"She believed you?"

"She *knows* I would! I'd cut the radio out too."

"Would you really have done that?"

"Yep. Revenge is *sweet*. I'm gonna take all my dad's tires off and *hide* 'em!"

CORNING

"Last night, we ran two and a half hours from people. We ran till four o'clock in the morning! We corned two cars!"

"What's *corning*? What does that mean?"

"Never ran so much in all my life!"

"You know that little house by the bridge? You go across that bridge, and the house is right there? Off them cliffs. We corned two cars."

"They drive by, and you throw corn on them?"

"Yeah."

"And you did that in the middle of the night?"

"The car was across the track. We had to go across the bridge cuz there was people walkin' around in the woods."

"Four o'clock in the morning???"

"Spotting deer."

"No! They were looking for *you*!"

"Yeah! You're goin' along, and this spotlight comes on. I never saw a kid move so quick! Just about got killed."

"So how did you get to your car?"

"My house—about three miles away. Took a half hour to get there!"

"Then you drove back and picked up your car."

"Yeah."

"All this is in the middle of the night? When was this?"

"Saturday night."

"Does corn hurt anything? You can still see. It doesn't stain? Doesn't break any windows?"

"Depends on how many people there are. It *has*."

"There were probably about forty or fifty of us! Remember that time all the cops came? Staties down in the next town! Everybody! Boy! They had us surrounded!"

"Coming after *you*?"

"Yeah! Staties! Town cops!"

"For throwing *corn*?"

"Yep. It was on the scanner. We come down, we jumped down over a road, we jumped down a bank, and we ran across the dam. Got away from them. There was about thirty or forty kids up there, an' nobody got caught!"

"You don't aim at any certain person. Whoever comes along gets it?"

"Yeah."

THESE WERE THE IRRESPONSIBLE ONES

There were at least a dozen people there with me, in the guidance office, seated around two conference tables pulled together to make one large, square table. They told me they could "fill a page" with complaints about school. There was nothing they liked about it. They were here with me because their guidance counselor said they were the worst, most hopeless students the school had. They would never graduate. They were always in detention. They didn't apply themselves in class. They were angry, defiant, uncooperative, rude, immature, irresponsible.

I had them for two full class periods without a break. At no time did they behave in a defiant, uncooperative, rude, immature, irresponsible way. They listened patiently and respectfully to each other and to me. They stayed on task the entire time. They did not show any signs that they were bored.

And this was what they said, the first time I met them.

Teachers shouldn't treat students as if they were "a group," as if they should have the same interests and the same abilities as their older brothers and sisters. They should get rid of homework, have classes from nine until two, give students some time out of school to earn some money, save some money, have a life. Teachers were too bossy. They didn't understand why more of them couldn't be nice. Some of them were nice. They didn't have any problem with those. It was the ones who said smart-aleck things to them, and then gave them detentions if they said smart-aleck things back. They said kids had no respect, but really it was the teachers who had no respect for students. If they did, they would see them as individuals, treat them as individuals.

It would help if teachers were patient, if they understood what it was like to learn something for the first time, if they didn't ridicule them for not understanding something, if they didn't assume that they didn't get it because they weren't paying attention. What school was was a time when teachers did all the talking all day long, and the students took notes. It would help if classes were only half an hour long. That should be long enough for teachers to talk, to tell them what to do. Half an hour long, five hours a day maximum, six months a year. It would balance out, give them a life half of every year. They could put up with it then.

The trouble was, you could change the school day. You could change the year. But you could never change the teachers—or the rest of the students. The friendly ones would always be friendly, and the boring ones would always be boring, and the rude ones would always be rude. Sometimes it was the students that made life uncomfortable and sad— because some of them had a lot of money, and when you didn't have any, you felt bad. The ones with the money acted like they were better than you were. They acted like you shouldn't even say hi to them. "Who are *you*?!" That's how they acted. "Who are *you*, that you should say hi to *me*? Don't you know that I have more money than you? Don't you know I'm better than you?"

Sometimes they thought all teachers were alike, thought they all had an attitude problem, thought they all got on kids' nerves. The teachers said it was the students who had "an attitude problem," but it was the teachers, really. It just seemed like they didn't care how you felt. It just seemed like teachers thought they knew everything. It seemed like they were never wrong. If you questioned them, they had a smart comeback. They had to have *some* kind of comeback. They always got the last word. And then you were left sitting there, feeling stupid. They could be irritated with you. They could have bad days. But you weren't enti- tled to bad days. *You* were supposed to keep your feelings to yourself. "Keep your bad days to yourself!" That's how it was. You just couldn't trust teachers to treat you like a human being.

If they could, they'd quit school altogether. They still might. They knew people who had straight A's in high school, who couldn't get de- cent jobs, who worked in a factory, who had babies, who couldn't afford to go to college, who didn't know how you could do that, where you could leave the baby. They didn't want to leave the baby. They knew it would be easier for them, though, if they stayed in school and graduated. It was just that—how could you stick it out that long? They were only in tenth grade. How could they possibly do it? How could they keep coming, day after day, year after year, when no one listened to them, when no one understood how they felt, when no one treated them with respect, when nothing that happened in class was ever interesting, when they didn't understand what the teacher said, when they never had a break, when they never got a chance to discuss what they were learning—or not learning, when teachers talked all day, when they sent homework home every day, when every day was the same monotonous and meaningless and lonely routine? How could they possibly do that, without ever once expressing how angry they felt, without feeling like adults were really listening, without feeling like somebody really cared that that's how it was for them? What was it like when *you* were in high school? Did you like *your* teachers? Were they *nice*? Were your classes *interesting*? Don't you remember? Don't you remember? Don't you remember?

WHO'S GOING TO HEAR YOU WHEN YOU TALK?

At one school I visited, every student in my group but one had dropped out—and now he was getting ready to drop out too. The teachers thought it was funny. They laughed when I talked to them. One told me he had half a dozen kids in one class, sleeping every day. He figured they were just losers, just lazy, just didn't want to bother to learn anything.

The principal saw it that way too, thought he stayed up late watching television, thought he stayed up because it was fun. The marking period ended in two weeks. At that time, the guidance counselor was going to recommend that he drop out, go to night school two hours a night, two nights a week, finish up that way. The student didn't know what was going to happen to him, couldn't imagine going to night school, didn't know what you could do without a high school diploma. His parents didn't come to the school, didn't talk to him, didn't talk to his teachers, figured it was his business, couldn't care less.

It was just that he felt like an orphan, felt like there was no one there to listen to him, no one to feed him when he was hungry, notice whether he was there or not, notice how he felt, care two cents how he felt. His father was abusive. He didn't want to be around his father. He found a second father, an old wood carver, used to help him, used to hang out in his workshop, even had a bed there, where he could spend the night when he wanted to. But the old man developed a brain tumor and was taken to the hospital. He went to visit him there, went over and over. The old man kept getting worse, got so he didn't know who he was any more. The old man died.

So he couldn't sleep, thinking about him, thinking about what was in store for him in his own life, now that there wasn't any place to go, any place where people cared. So he lay with his eyes closed, in the middle of the night, listening to Led Zeppelin. He had all nine Led Zeppelin tapes, plus the one from the movie. That one was two hours long. He didn't have the music on loud. He didn't disturb anybody. He just lay there and thought. He didn't get anywhere in his thinking.

He worked in a convenience store not far from home, worked twenty hours a week or more, worked Friday, Saturday, Sunday, and Monday, worked a lot for an eleventh grader, saved his money to buy Led Zeppelin tapes. His father used to listen to Led Zeppelin when he was younger. The last one he got cost nine-fifty. His English teacher told him to put it away in class one day, told him it wasn't appropriate to have it in class when he was supposed to be concentrating on English, told him in front of everyone: "Put it away. Concentrate. Do as you're told." He didn't put it away. She took it away from him and started crumpling it in her hand. She didn't have it folded up right—the little black piece of cardboard inside the tape box. It unfolds three times. The way she had it, she was practically crumpling it. He kept asking for it back, and she wouldn't give it to him, so he threatened to hit her. "Give it back! Please! It's my newest one! It cost nine-fifty!" Nothing doing. He said he'd hit her if she didn't give it back. He said it was his property. Seventeen-year-olds were entitled to their own property. She told him to go to the office, told him to tell them he was threatening a teacher. He went. As he walked out the door, he punched the door as hard as he could. She gave him his property back. They kicked him out for ten days. He said he didn't care. They could kick him out as many times as they wanted. It was his property. She shouldn't have taken it.

He was already in a bad mood because in homeroom he wouldn't say the Pledge of Allegiance. He stood up, he stood quietly, with his hands at his sides. The teacher sent him to the office, because he wouldn't say the Pledge of Allegiance. Jehovah's Witnesses didn't have to say the Pledge of Allegiance. They could walk right out of class when they said it. It was school policy. You didn't have to say it if you didn't believe in it. But the teacher didn't care about school policy. The teacher thought he should say it. He didn't want to say it, felt phony saying it. What had the United States of America ever done for him? The teacher told the principal that he wasn't quiet. He was quiet. It was the teacher's word against his. Wasn't he always quiet—in every class? Did he ever say anything? No, he didn't. He was invisible. He was invisible everywhere. Who was going to listen to him when he talked? Who was ever going to listen to him?

I JUST DON'T CONCENTRATE IN SCHOOL
NO MORE—I DON'T KNOW WHY

> When ya come to school the people look atcha like
> you was a fool.
> They takin' me to prison, I'm endin' like *this*—

Teachers were on their case. First period they had study hall, second period they had study hall, third period, swimming. It was because they kept messing around. One missed a whole *week*! One missed thirty times. To tell you the truth, out of the whole year, one came two days. He missed sixty-two days. He'd be the last person graduating. He never came to school. When he came to school, he didn't do his work. "You talk about my grades?" he said. "I be on drugs." His friend said he *sold* drugs, said his uncle was the king of the *Swat*. They were just playing around, see. They were just having fun. They laughed so hard they got tired.

You didn't have to raise your hand in gym. It made 'em mad to raise their hands. They were trying to hit the books. They just couldn't. It was a long story.

Their friends last period said we rapped for half an hour. They were impressed.

It was all on the tape. They wanted to be on the tape too.

You'd think it would be fun to be at school with your friends, but it was not fun. It was not fun *at all*! They wished it could be fun. It was sad.

School was *boring*. You had to be here too early. You had to be quiet in class. You weren't allowed to *talk*. You had to be very very quiet. Only time you didn't was when there was a cute substitute. Then you were like, drawing pictures, and doing raps, an' it was not so bad—only you weren't learning anything.

They were thinking about getting a publisher. They was gonna write a *book* about their lifestyle from seven to sixteen. It would be a best seller. It'd be crime and stuff, how they learned to do crime, how they started using drugs. It'd be real cool.

There oughta be more black girls, more pretty black girls, pretty white girls. There were too many prejudiced people. You know why they didn't like school? They were messing around.

All right, listen.

> I don't mean to be stupid to be at school,
> Goin' to school, just bein' bored.
> I'm tellin' you, you know,
> I want to go to school,
> but it's a chore.

> Outside it is cold and rainy. I'm hesitatin'.
> Want to stay at home and relax. Watch the TV.
> It's cool and nice. Relax. Chill.
> Lay on the couch. Turn on the stereo.

> Mom is goin' to work at eight.
> Eight o'clock comes. She is gone.

> Do you wanna skip school? Do you wanna play hookey?
> Let's have some cookies an' chill.

> Every mornin' at eight o'clock. My mom is gone.
> She's down the block. She turns the corner
> An' who do I see? None other than my old boy, D.D.
> He comes inside the house and he lays down.

> Cuz I know your style. He has a frown on his face.
> He's mad, cuz his dad woke him up.
> He wanta stay in bed.

My turn, he says. My turn. You just make it up as you go. My turn, he says. My turn.

> I stayed in bed. I was gonna be a fool.
> Cuz I never paid attention and I didn't go to school.
> I always paid attention, and I did not learn.
> I was always gettin' busted, and I had to burn.
> In history and math class, floatin' 'round my head,
> Things were goin' fast.
>
> I didn't have the time to pay attention.
> Spend my life in that detention. Yes!
> Cuz I was bad. I was feelin' blue.
> I was feelin' sad. Wanted to make love,
> But I didn't have time.
>
> I didn't want to go out and commit no crime.
> Me an' him just skip school.
> We sit here all day and talk on the phone.
> That's why we wasn't alone.
> I was with him, an' he was with me.
> We never with the school, as you can see.
> We were passin'. We're failin' now.
>
> I feel, yes, very sad, with my dad.
> Just feel so bad.
> One day my dad got mad, and kicked me out,
> And I felt real sad.
> He kicked me to the curb. I had nowhere to go.
> I wish I went to school. Now I am *gone*.

So they skipped study hall. Two study halls in a row—why not? They used to go to all their classes, but they just didn't concentrate in school no more. They didn't know why. It was the environment. They couldn't do no homework. They thought they would, but they would not do it. They would lay down and sleep all the way till eleven o'clock, and get up, and look at the time, and they would not do the homework.

What if they were the parents? And their kids were doing the same things they were doing? They'd get a tutor. They'd do something one on one. If they hit the books, they'd get a reward. But that don't work. One dad offered his son a car already. That should make you work, but he still didn't work. He could get anything he wanted. He wasn't living like he was poor. They had the middle class. You know what they're saying? Sometimes they tried, and sometimes they didn't try. Like today. They didn't want to come to school. They weren't gonna come. But they came, because they got in trouble and missed a couple days. Couldn't remember what day it was. Came because they missed all last week. Why did they come? They didn't give you no second chance at school. They didn't give you no individual attention. The counselor came down, and the counselor said, "You missed this *class!*" The counselor did the talking, chewed them out. Naw! *They* didn't get to talk. They'd just be staring out the window.

HEY! WHERE'D YOU GET THAT GOLD?

"They shoulda stayed outta the game."

A student

So they both knew where they were taking themselves, and they went there anyway, and nobody knows where they are now, ten years later. They disappeared from the scene. They're gone. I hope their mothers and girlfriends know what *mea culpa* means. I hope they look in the mirror every morning, and every night before they go to bed, after they count up all the call waiting and call forwarding expenses and all the jewels and all the cars and all the nice clothes that came from their sons' doings and their boyfriends', and all the pretending that nothing is wrong, and that it's none of their responsibility, and that guilt is the same as innocence, really, and say the only prayer that makes any sense of it: *mea culpa, mea culpa, mea culpa!* And I hope their fathers understand how large a hole they left in their sons' lives when they turned their backs on them. And I hope their schools are ashamed, not of these two boys, who are legion, but of themselves, for alternately walking away from them and pushing them faster and more chaotically down the slippery slope they slid down. And I hope their friends are safe, wherever they are. And I hope some day we all say, "These are *our* kids, *our* kids, *our* kids, *our* kids. My God, My God, *why* have we forsaken them?"

You see, the others laughed. They laughed a painful, nightmarish, embarrassed, aware, older than seventeen laugh. They laughed because those two got caught.

"They shoulda stayed outta the game!" they said—the game of not coming to school, the game of getting in too deep, the game of being taken in by all that glitters in the name of gold.

One of them was in prison. The other was in another institution somewhere. I got the name of it from the guidance counselor, called, learned that there were privacy laws, and that they might not say whether he was there or whether he wasn't.

I tried to explain. But what if his mother was on drugs and his father didn't talk, and what if we were his only real friends, and what if we didn't want him to think that we had abandoned him? What then? What good was his privacy if he was drowning in it? We were afraid for him. He needed to know we cared. He needed to know we remembered what his dream was. We wanted him to have real ground under his feet. We knew there was no ground there now. We knew they didn't speak any mutually understandable language at his house. We knew they couldn't listen to each other. We knew there was too much anger there, and too much hurt there, to listen. You have to have some hope to listen, and they had run out of hope at his house.

"Well," she said, "If you put it that way, then by all means, send your cards and letters. If you think he's here, then send them, and we will see that he gets them, if he's here."

It was the last we heard from her or him. He was *gone*, just as he said he was. We knew that. We just didn't want to believe it.

As for the other one, he was caught selling his soul for a little cash to impress the girls he knew. He knew the wrong girls. We knew that. He knew the wrong girls, but they didn't know him. They were looking in the mirror. There was only room there for their empty eyes, and the cash, and the gold, and the diamonds. They thought it was cool, having all that.

So he spent his senior year in a place that looked like a college if you didn't open your eyes wide—nice clean bricks stacked up in nice clean boxes, and nice green grass, and nice little houses with a real mother and a real father that were actually married to each other and that actually lived in the same house and actually lived there every day and actually set some limits that had to be lived with, that were supposed to set an example of sensible and safe living, so that when they got out, those boys in bunk beds, two to a room like some sad Noah's ark escaping from the flood of everything they knew about the universe, they would themselves be sensible and safe, and raise sensible and safe children forever.

But while he was there, they forgot. They allowed him to go home, visit whatever tattered remains there were of what they still called a family, allowed him to go back into the neighborhood he had so recently left, stuff his pockets with whatever he stuffed them with before, bring it all back to his new neighborhood of clean and tidy bricks and freshly cut grass with no beer cans and bottles and used-up cigarettes in it, and no McDonald's and Burger King hamburger wrappers in it, and no blood, and hopefully no knives and guns.

So they had him in something like solitary confinement now, which was not really solitary confinement, which was just a place where nobody else was, so he could think about what he had done, and what he should have done, and take some fraction of responsibility for it, which he did not want to take, because even the smallest fraction of it was too large to comprehend for him, who had no idea where responsibility might lead, who did not expect it to lead to any impressive, glamorous, or comfortable destination, who thought responsibility must be a drag, must be a disappointment the size of the Pacific Ocean compared with having your name spoken in secretly admiring whispers by everyone you knew under the age of eighteen and over the age of seventeen in your high school and on your street back home.

"Yeah! We *knew* him!" they all said. "We *knew* him!"

They said it like he was dead.

He dared to go after his dreams—that's how he looked at it—no matter how short-sighted his dreams were. He was trying to compensate for that granite tumor of hopelessness inside himself that he'd carried in there every year since he was a small child, since his father had left, and since he had been sent from one relative to another, one city, one state, to another, to whoever would take him for a while—as if he were just baggage that kept getting sent to the wrong address.

Those short-sighted dreams will live on. You can't kill them with a little solitary confinement. After all, you could say he's had a whole life of solitary confinement, shut off from all sanity and sense, shut off from all nurturing and compassion and all insight and good judgment and all guidance that really does guide.

I asked him once if he had ever heard of an *old* drug dealer.

"Oh," he said. "Like forty? Naw! There *aren't* any old drug dealers. They all die young."

MOST OF THEM ARE JUST A PAIN IN THE ASS

It seems like they're just here to earn their paycheck—except the science teacher, and the principal, and one or two others.

You almost gotta be friends. Teachers that are more or less friends give a little leeway—a little jokin' here and there, you know—and don't take everything so personal, get more respect from students than teachers that are awful mean, and strict, and everything. I mean, if I'm his friend, I wouldn't want to do anything to my buddy here. I wouldn't like him if he was always mean to me. I'd get back at him. And that's the way I look at teachers.

Anymore, teachers *demand* respect, but you gotta *earn* it. If you *demand* it, you ain't gonna *get* respect. You can't hold something against kids all the time. Teachers threatening you all the time, threatening you about sports. They threaten you with pink slips. They threaten you with in-school suspension.

They're holdin' it over our head all the time. "Okay! You got ISS!" They're always threatening kids. They just go around saying "I'll smash your face" and stuff. Maybe all the kid said was "I like your hair." It was a compliment. And the teacher says, "Don't talk to me like that! I'll hit you in the face!"

They're always saying "Start actin' your *age!*" And we're like, "Sure! As soon as you start *treatin'* us our age!"

At Vo-Tech, it's different. We're up there to see what the world is, so they're going to teach us, like, what our age is.

I can't wait to get back to shop. Sometimes it's boring—especially when you get a hard job. Sometimes you have trouble finding something, when it's a hard job. Every time, when I work, I go home and think about it. Like one time, I did this rocker panel. And I couldn't do it in one piece of metal. You have to cut it. So I tried to prove him wrong. I was doin' good and stuff, you know. But I forgot—I didn't have my metal bent straight, and I worked on it real bad. He knew I did it wrong, but he didn't say nothin', cuz he wanted me to find out for myself. Cuz I was sure I could do it. He'll do that type of thing. He'll wait. And he'll say, "You wanted to try it, but it didn't work." What happened was, if you shut the door, the edge of it came out too far. And then he came over, and he caught it, and he improved it, and he did a little bit of it, and he goes, "See *that*?" He shows you what you did wrong.

At regular school, the teachers talk all the time. Or they'll ask a question and some student will answer it. Most of the time, they're just bossin' us around.

They just want us to shut up. Some kids are sent to ISS three or four times a day.

But the principal is cool. He's probably one of the best teachers. You know, he gets down there and wrestles with the wrestlers and everything else. He's not one of those stuffed-shirt principals that sits in his office all day and reads the newspaper! You see him all over the place. Saw him this morning. He's like, "What are *you* guys up to?" He wants to know and stuff.

Most of the time, teachers say something—we have a teacher, smart ass, he'll say something—to get in an argument. His way or no way. He's been workin' here since the school was built. They think they can hold these pink slips over our heads, but anymore it doesn't bother us. It means ISS. If you don't take it, you get three days out. Yep, three days out. And pretty soon, it's summertime.

If you stand up for yourself in school, they don't like you. They just jump up and talk the whole period about how bad we are. I had a teacher in eighth grade. She said, "Oh, you'll be sorry. You'll get to high school, and you'll never make it." And I'm graduatin'.

High school is bad, but it's a lot better than middle school. Middle school—there's a bunch of ancient people there, about a hundred. It's only one way, and that's the forties! They don't listen. They don't like to change. They used to bug me about my hair. I had long hair.

I wear a lot of jackets and stuff. And there's this one teacher—I went to talk to one of the girls that was in her homeroom, and she took her right back inside. Didn't want her talkin' to me, cuz of the way I dressed.

Teachers go by the hair, you know. They go by your hair and your family. If they know your parents are doin' bad, they're down on *you*.

Same with my brother. They get on me cuz my one brother was always in trouble.

One thing that bothers me is that the teachers go to college, and they think there's no more to learn. You know, we can still teach *them* things — things they've never come across. They don't see it that way. They can't learn no more. They're the smartest. They know more than we do. It makes me so mad. A few months ago, I got in all kinds of trouble in the lunch line. I told the freshmen, "I was in school longer than you was, so I should be able to budge in front of you." And yesterday, one of the teachers was in line, and he budged in in front of *us*. Like he should have to wait like everybody else. He goes, "That's what authority does for you!" We been here longer than he has! Why should teachers be able to do that?

Teachers get out of college and think there isn't any more learning involved. A lot of people still learn things. At these big institutes and stuff, they'll be teachin' other people how to play the guitar, and they'll learn from *them*. I'm sure there will be teachers who don't know how to play melodies and stuff, and I know how to play classical.

Teachers think they just can't learn any more. They're *smart*. Their brain's filled *up*. That's *wrong*!

It's hard to learn something, especially when somebody tells you how to do things, and you *know* it. My little brother asks me how to do something, and I say, "No, you gotta do it this way," and I might sound like one of these teachers.

My dad's real smart. He makes a joke of it. He makes it light. He doesn't rub it in.

Yesterday, the teacher took my homework and lost it, and he never said he did. And he looked at my book and he picked it up, and everybody seen him there, and I turned my head and the book was gone. And I'm like, "What did you do with my book?" And he's like, "I never touched it." He forgot he gave it to my buddy to get some pages copied. And he's, "Oh, that's right." Things like that really count.

Like I had a lot of work done one time, and he lost it, and he never said that's what he did. It's things like that that really bug you, cuz they expect responsibility out of you: "Bring your *book*," and stuff.

But they can't admit it when they make a mistake.

I hate these people: "Gee, I wish I was still in school!" My sister said that the other day, and I got so mad. I said, "Bullcrap!" I said, "You know how it is. Really down deep, ain't it nice that you have your own home? You don't have to worry about people tellin' you to shut up, and do this, and do that?' And she says, "Well, yeah, that's true." I hate that. You can't tell me you miss school, sittin' in class, listenin' to a teacher talk all day! How can you *miss* it?

STUPID PEANUT HEADS

We can't stand it, because teachers, they ignore you. They waste your time. And there's a lot of preppy peanut heads in this school. You know, teachers need to get more respect for the students, cuz there's a lot of prejudice in the school. They try to hide it, you know, but you can't hide nothin' in this world! You know, you can't have no prejudices in school!

Most of the students in this school get a lot of respect because of what color they are, or who they're goin' out with in this school. You know, I can walk through the halls. I'm not supposed to walk through the halls or go to my locker. I'm not supposed to. And I go anyway. Let somebody else do that, and they go, "Oh, it's *all right* for *you* to do it." But when I go to my locker, it's "Oh, *you're* not *allowed* to do that, and you *know* you're not allowed to do that."

Most of these teachers around here don't like you just because of some of the things you did last year. But it's a brand new year! You're supposed to start all over!

A preppie is a person who's a snob. They always dress the right way. They're never wrong. A lot of people in this school are preppies be-cause their parents have a lot of money, and if you want to be different, and do your own thing, then people look down on you, and they spread rumors about you.

I think a preppy, to tell you the truth, is a person that thinks they're too high-class—the way they talk, the way they act. I think more preppy people are ignorant-type people.

Not all the preps are ignorant, just the people who are in like, honors classes. Most of those people that are in honors class, those kind of preppies are like the snobby preppies. They think they're better than everyone.

The most majority of people that goes here is *white* people. And they don't get into as much trouble because of the kind of person they are. Because they choose people by the color of their skin. They do things for, say things for, take up for this student and that—white, black, Puerto Rican, purple, blurple, whatever. They pick favorites. And then teachers are smart with you and everything, and you get detention.

Like when they call you stupid peanut head names. And they call you *boy!* The teacher likes that word, *boy!* You use that word way way back in the days when people was pickin' cotton. It's not one of them words that you want to use, because he's goin' to call somebody a boy one more time. You'll say something, and he'll ask you what did you say, and when you say it, he'll give you a detention.

If you have a problem, and you're in pain, the nurse'll set you down, go through how many times you were absent, take your temperature, and say, "What's the problem?" The problem is my stomach hurts. "Well, what *organ* hurts?" I don't know what an organ is! So, if you don't have an answer, she goes, "Well, I don't really think you're sick!" And then you say, "Well, I want to go home! And if I get sick they send me home." "Well, I don't think you should go home, cuz you were absent ten days." She'll send you back to your class, and you'll be in pain and everything. If you go down to the other office, and tell them you want to go home, she says, "Well, we won't send you home any more." And you could have cramps.

I get the cramps real bad, and when I get them, I start to throw up and stuff. She told me, "No, you're not supposed to do that!" Every girl in this school is different. Every boy in this school is different. She cannot sit and tell me how I'm supposed to get sick. She wouldn't send me home, cuz I got real sick. I went to the office and said, "I want to go home, cuz I'm real sick," and they wouldn't let me go home, so I skipped a class and I went down here, and I called almost everybody in my family so I could get in touch with my mom so she would come and pick me up. And she asked me, "Don't you like this school?" I said, "What's it to you? You ain't no teacher. Why do you have to know if I like school or not?" And she goes, "Well, you missed so and so, such a many days."

We pay like, three thousand dollars a whole year's school now. Well, actually, that's a lot of money just for goin' to high school. We don't got respect, we don't got no kind o' respect. I mean, Catholics pay half price. It come down to it, everybody believes in the same God—Baptist, Catholic. I think all Catholics should have to pay the same amount as non-Catholics.

When you walk around here, you can tell the rich ones from the non-rich. These are the ones that make sports, I'm tellin' ya. I played basketball for another school, and we were really good. I know I shouldn't say that. Anyway, we went out for the team, and we were only on it for like a week, and he like, already knew his favorites. They'd be slack and everything, and he'd push us harder than he pushed them. All the teachers do. They have their favorites. They get away with everything. Someone had cocaine, and they didn't even get the cops in here. Then last year, they talked about gettin' in people's lockers and takin' people's coats, and they were tryin' to say that I was the one takin' their coats. Well, I could buy this whole school a coat. How do you like that?! I'm not prejudiced or nothing, but if you look at it, there's more white people that cause trouble than black people, but when the black people do something, they're harder on them.

The ones that are gettin' counseled get blamed. When you are here being counseled and everything, it doesn't mean you're havin' trouble. But they're gonna ask you, "Are you having trouble at home?" No! I have no trouble. If I had so much trouble, I wouldn't be in this school. I'd be on the street someplace. Because they think that I'm gonna cut up! Problems at home! No! And they want to know your whole life story!

They say, "Oh! You must be havin' trouble at *home!*" His parents are divorced! Or her parents don't *love* her, or something like that.

When you get in trouble, that's the first thing! "Well, how's your mother and your father?" I'm like, "They're here for *their* education! I'm here for *mine!* So don't worry about my mom and dad!" You try to talk to the counselor, do something to help you. They go, "I understand." No! You *don't* understand!

Here I am in this room with this guy. I'm sittin' all the way at the other end of the room. It's crazy. He's like, "What's your *problem?!*" I mean, you can go over there right now. You'll see one chair at the other end. He sits on this end. You sit all the way at the other end. And he's just lookin' out the window, and not even payin' attention to you. He's like, "Oh! Are you *upset?*"

WHY DON'T THEY JUST UNDERSTAND?

This is prison. They're supposed to be havin' some drug dogs runnin' around!

This morning, he tried to say that we didn't dress very good, and we dress the best in the area! I mean, *any* school! Guys come in school without their ties and with sneakers on. And they're gettin' on the girls about shorts and miniskirts.

I'm down at the office, cuz this kid is throwin' BBs, right? And I got in trouble for it, cuz of one lousy BB. And I'm sittin' there, and he says, "Send him in," and this town police cop walked right in the door. I didn't know what I was in there for. Turned out he was in there for a traffic ticket out front! Somebody parked wrong! Somebody told me they heard I was doin' drugs, or dealin'. They got the wrong people! They got *somebody*. They just had locker searches and stuff. They had 'em in the office. He's like, "Get 'em in there!" And they had to take their shoes off! Take their ties off. They had to strip down almost completely. That ain't right!

You don't have to do *anything*—you get in trouble. Like if you're late for school, you get a detention, and if you don't go to detention, you get out-of-school suspension. He yelled at me yesterday because I had my Walkman—after school, and I was just about to leave. I had it on, and he told me to turn it off, and I said, "No!" Then he started yellin' at me, and he almost broke it. Then they're sayin' I was the one at fault there.

This kid carved his name in a desk. It was new. It wasn't there when I first went there. So I put my name in beside it. So, like a month later, I'm called down to the office, and I get in trouble for it. Just because they don't like *me*, I got in trouble for it, not the other guy. You know what the punishment was? I had to clean with the janitors, scrapin' the gum off with a spatula, man. I was pickin' it up and flingin' it at the girls playin' basketball. I was supposed to be doin' it for a week, but I never went back. One day was enough for me!

I don't know if you heard about this, but this girl got drunk, like in the school dance. She was drunk as anything could be, right? She threw up and everything else! And they catch her, you know? Cuz she's throwin' up. They believe *her*, you know? They said, "Where did you get it from?" And she said that I was *with* her, which I was *with* her, but

I wasn't drunk. They got me at the dance. I wasn't *drunk*—right? Nothin' like that. Well, they had the police and everything. I passed every test they gave me, like walkin' lines. And this girl says, "He was *with* me!" The girl got three days' suspension for *double* what I did, and I got three days' suspension too. Was *that* right?! She comes in, double what I was—and I get the same punishment!

Check *this* out! The nurse. I was sick as a dog! She won't send me home from school! I had a fever. Last year, I went to the nurse. I had pink eye, and she wouldn't send me home.

We go to this Catholic dump because we're not goin' to the public school. It's a massacre up there.

They beat up on the teachers up there.

The principal got beat up, like two or three times this year. A couple of teachers I know got dropped off. They use that as a threat to us. They say, I'm sittin' in their office, right? They say, "Well, you gonna tell us everything that happened?" And I say, "I ain't tellin' on nobody." And I was sittin' there, and they say, "You wanta go to this school anymore, you're gonna tell us." They say, "This is a private school. We can just put you right outa here! Right up to the public school!" They use that like blackmail.

This one teacher is always sendin' home letters: "He's flunkin' this class! He has one more chance to make up!" And all the time, they send home letters: "He has one more chance. He has one more chance." And, if you get in trouble, they tell the whole school. So-and-so has detention today.

That's exactly what they say: "So-and-so report to the attendance office immediately." They called me down the other day, and everybody came up to me: "I heard you got busted for *drugs*!"

That's what gets me mad. When they want to see you, all they have to do is send a slip to you. If you want to see *them*, they're always in a meeting! When they want to give you detention, they find you. But when you gotta go talk to them about a problem you got, like if you want to change your detention, you can never find them. And if you're not there for detention, you gotta take *two* of them. They're like, "Why didn't you call me?" "Well, I couldn't find you." And they're like: "That's just an excuse. I don't want to hear about it. I don't want to talk about it anymore!"

Why don't they just understand that kids gotta get their way a little bit too?

NINTH GRADE

I like my hair at times, and my taste. I don't like my weight, my freckles, my geometry grades, my hair at times, or my body, sometimes.

My mother thinks that I am basically the opposite of what I really am.

My father thinks I don't know about sex, drugs, world problems, and how to handle myself as a mature adult person. He thinks I'm dumb, unknowing, innocent, and a pain in the ass.

When I'm happy, I usually smile and laugh, and get in trouble for laughing. When I'm unhappy, I sometimes cry and get into verbal and physical fights.

Sometimes people don't like me when I am ignorant, bitchy, and tired.

It's hard to like myself when I'm in a bad mood, or when a relationship doesn't work out.

I usually tell myself about having the will to live, or the will to survive.

I think it's hard to understand men.

Sometimes I get worried when someone I care for gets hurt, or someone is missing, or when I hurt someone I love (or at least think I hurt them).

I wish my life (regular and love) would improve severely or end totally.

I wonder why life stinks so much, and why some teachers are employed, and why I have bad luck all the time.

When I think about life, I am filled with wonder. Sometimes I love it and never want it to stop. Then there are days, a great many at times, when I wish to end it quicker than physically possible.

WHEN I THINK ABOUT TENTH GRADE

When I think about tenth grade, I guess I mostly feel scared. I feel scared because it means another year has gone by that I've mostly missed. What I mean is that the past few school years have just gone *zip*! It started at the end of seventh grade. My friends and I couldn't believe how fast the year had gone. And then eighth went even faster. And ninth has gone about twice as fast as either.

So I'm sort of scared because if the years keep flying by this fast, the next thing I know it's going to be graduation, [and] I'll be picking colleges, and going out on my own to the real world. I find that pretty frightening. There are just so many things I want to do before then, and it seems like it's all coming up too quickly and I'm going to be lost in it all.

FOURTEEN

When I think about life it seems to me that it's OK until a certain point, like I'm not afraid to die but I'm afraid to get really old. Like there's *some* cool old people but the majority are just there—they can't do much for themselves and they don't do any good, and most seem like they are unhappy with life so why don't they just die?!? I know that I want to die before I'm 50 or 60. I think that's a full enough life. Life kind of is frightening at times but basically it's OK, just like don't waste it. See my views seem almost contradictory—I want to die early, yet I feel life is something you gotta do something with (constructively)—so do what you want as long as it makes you happy but when it doesn't keep you happy then you die. Life is a gift and if it ceases to bring you enjoyment then you can just simply return it! . . .

CHAPTER 5

"Poetry, Like Bread, Is for Everyone":
Breaking Down Stereotypes

"POETRY, LIKE BREAD, IS FOR EVERYONE"

"I believe the world is beautiful
and that poetry, like bread, is for everyone.

Roque Dalton, "Like You"

When I graduated from college, a classmate gave me a copy of Edward Steichen's photograph collection, *The Family of Man.* I page through it now: the pages of Italian lovers, and New Guinea lovers, and English lovers, and American lovers, and French lovers; the marriages in Japan, in Czechoslovakia, in India, in Sweden, in Mexico; the pregnancies, the labor, the births, the sleeping infants, the wailing infants, the mother resting her face on the bed, the infant learning this game of warm glances, the cat on the bed, watching. China, Guatemala, Russia—the same. The wealthy, the poor, the same. The world's children walking, writing, leaping, marching, shouting, splashing, clowning, laughing, playing.

We trade places, in the photographs, move up, move out of the picture, are replaced by others who move up, and out. We ride the crest of the wave, and go down. Ride, and go down.

When I visit city schools, I think of these things. Somehow, in the country, the wave seems not to be a wave; the crest is only a ripple. In the country, we move at the speed of corn. Every day we walk, jog, drive, bicycle past the same field, watch the plowing, the planting, see the first shoots come up, go about our business, forget the calendar, drive up the same hill day after day without seeing—our minds on our business. Corn may rise relentlessly, may shoot past us, be reduced to stubble while we sleep, but the reassuring field lies bare again, presents an opportunity for us to see again—until decades go by, and we see.

In the city, there is no corn to measure by, no cycle, no second chance. There is only the traffic, and the trash, and the sense that something immeasurably large has been lost. Those of us from the country see the city in this way, have not learned to see past the noise and the dirty air, past the anonymity and the hunger, past the need and the empty hands. We do not find it beautiful, do not know how to call this chronic waste and neglect and inefficiency and indifference and decay beautiful.

Those who come from the city find our corn pace boring. Nothing happens, they say. And you feel too vulnerable, too open, too exposed, too alone, too lonely.

We are of two different habits. We share no language, no experience. Where can we begin? What shall we speak about?

"Visit *my* school!" says one student.

"No! Visit *mine*!"

"No! *Mine*!"

I choose one, walk into the school unannounced, schedule an appointment with the English chair, the science chair, the guidance counselor, arrange to visit ninth graders, eleventh graders, seniors, to read papers, follow along on textbook assignments, listen to classroom discussion, occasionally take over the class for conversations about college. Sometimes three or four college students meet me at six o'clock in the morning to make the long trip down. We divide the class into discussion groups. Each of us leads one. My students tell the younger ones what college life is like: not good. Nothing to do up there. Boring classes. Nothing worth learning. Not enough diversity. Why are they there, then? They laugh. Too late to transfer, they say. They'd lose their credits.

The younger students like this sassy, unsubtle criticism. These visits are festive occasions, suspenseful. Truths have a way of slipping in, truths punctuated with unselfconscious, mischievous laughter.

After a morning of classes, we accompany the teachers to the faculty dining room, listen to their side of things, find out what renews their spirits, are surprised to find that they listen to each other, sympathize, empathize, stay abreast of every crisis, every lapse of sense in the system.

Life is not like this, where the corn grows. Sympathy and humor don't grow well there, don't take root. Here, where so much is lacking, humanity grows strong, waters everything that needs attention with encouragement and laughter. It's the system, they say. You *have* to laugh. There's no other way to beat it. You either leave, or you laugh.

In the spring, we invite the younger students and their teachers to visit the college, organize a panel discussion focused on what high school students need to do, now, to prepare for the careers they want. College students escort their guests to lunch in the dining hall, accompany them to workshops in photography, outdoor adventure/teamwork, painting, dance, interactive video. They tour our radio and television studio.

The high school students had never been to this college, had never heard of it, had never been to any predominantly white campus surrounded by a predominantly white town. They like these green hills, like the adventure of being the visitors, have some idea, now, how far we might travel together.

THINKING ABOUT THE BEAUTY OF PLACE

It startles me to realize that I have never seen a beautiful school — anywhere. I sit here, now, at my computer, staring out into the dark hundred-foot fir trees on my neighbor's undeveloped property, open the door, listen to the breeze a hundred feet over my head. Breezes here are rare. Breezes mean rain is coming, will probably be here by morning. Today the wind has brought dozens of birds. Stellar jays guard the feeder, swoop up and down in front of my window all afternoon. Robins and other brown birds pick at the dirt in the front garden. I stand watching them, brown bits of mulch in motion — that's how they look from this distance. They dart back and forth as if they had never seen this vast dinner plate before, as if they'd been planning a trip here for weeks, and just can't get over the abundance of it all. There must be twenty, thirty, of them out there. The ground is covered with them.

You don't see anything like this from a schoolroom window. Kids don't get a chance to discover that the wind is blowing, don't watch birds. They're busy learning. Their windows look out on parking lots and paved playgrounds. Their air is all stale, recycled air.

I don't know what a beautiful school would look like, exactly, but it wouldn't look institutional. It wouldn't look like a cross between a prison and a fall-out shelter, or a warehouse. It wouldn't look cheap. It wouldn't be built with huge slabs of concrete and wallboard. It wouldn't consist of rows and rows of identical rooms, and identical hallways, and identical lockers, and identical lights, and identical chairs and tables. It wouldn't have windows that didn't open.

The windows that it had would have a view that was worth looking at: water, hills, sky, winding paths, birds, animals, gardens that didn't look like any other gardens anywhere, people doing interesting one-of-a-kind things—Henry Moore, working on a bronze sculpture; his wife, planting blueberries and butterfly bushes; Langston Hughes, writing poems; my mother's Swedish cousin, weaving her own area rug; Vladimir Horowitz, playing the piano—everywhere, creators creating, without haste, without transcripts and grades, without in-school suspension, without policemen at the door.

"School!" It would be a place where people of all ages could hardly wait to go, a place where they taught, and learned from, each other, a place where each person decided for him- or herself what to learn and when to learn it, and what to do with the consequences of the learning. "School!" It would be like a Barnes and Noble Bookstore—with over-stuffed chairs near all the best books, and thirty-inch square tables, with parents and children and carpenters and printers and wrestlers and loggers reading newspapers, and sipping morning coffee, and milk.

It would be like a YMCA, with an exercise room, and a pool, where parents and grandparents and children and teenagers swam laps, and worked out, or planned water ballets, or trained for the Olympics. It would be like the public library, where they signed in with their library card, to use the computers for an hour, to read newspapers and magazines. It would be like the Geology Club that sponsors junior members and takes them out to remote river beds to hunt for fossils all afternoon, like a Fall Festival of marching bands, and poetry readings, and painting exhibits, and pottery workshops.

What *couldn't* it be? How human a place we could build—if we could make schools to fit the greatest interests and the greatest needs of the individuals and the communities that require and support them.

Oh, the schools I've visited were never like that, even in elementary and middle schools! I never saw kids "just being kids." I never saw kids with their families. I never saw them working together to dream, to design, to invent. Even in third grade, I saw tense, anxious, preoccupied children, trying to pay attention, filling in blanks, taking tests, copying spelling words, working, working, working—performing, performing, performing—all of it pure drudgery. I saw classrooms where looking out the window was an offense that met with a reprimand, or even a punishment. I saw classrooms where getting out of your seat to "stretch your legs" was a sign of your inability to focus, a sign of your unwillingness to abide by the teacher's rules. I saw classrooms where learning was grim business. Almost everywhere I looked, in thirty years, it seemed as if schools were taking the life out of kids, and showing them that engagement and value and discovery and eagerness and beauty and delight belonged—well, somewhere else, but certainly not in a school!

The city school was depressing in a new way—all the more eerie because no one there ever mentioned it. The city school was dirty and ugly. In the faculty parking lot, weeds grew in the cracks, and there was hardly a section of concrete that was not full of broken glass. The huge "lawn" was full of weeds and trash, the single, huge, red brick building covered with black graffiti.

On the street side, there were no windows. Three thousand students and several hundred faculty and staff passed between two rows of cyclone fencing, entered the building through only one of the dozens of ugly, graffiti-covered steel doors, and lined up at a makeshift checkpoint just inside.

"Sign your name here. State the nature of your business here, your destination here, the company you represent here. Please wear this tag. Thank you. Sign your name here. State the nature of your business here, your . . . Thank you." All day long, the security guards sat, or stood, in their dark hallway, their hallway with no windows, and no light, and no paintings on the walls, and no plants growing, and no music playing. All day long, they pointed out the location of the office at the far end of that long, dark tunnel.

Behind the counter, in the office, were at least half a dozen desks, not one of them occupied, even at the beginning of the school day. No one anywhere seemed to have the slightest interest in anyone who might be entering or standing at the counter. When I arrived there, I felt as if I were boarding a ship and finding out that the ship had no captain and no crew, though it had already set sail for somewhere. Arriving there, I felt, on every visit, that I had stepped into a floating fall-out shelter. But where it was going, and what protection it was offering, I never could tell.

SQUARE ROOTS OF MINUS NUMBERS

No matter when I arrived at the city school, there were always little clusters of people lounging outside—in the parking lot, on the sidewalk, by the door, just inside the door. When I asked the checkpoint crew why these people never came in, they told me they were students from other schools, skipping class, and most of them knew better than to try to come in. A few times, I arrived as they tried to persuade the checkpoint crew that they had some urgent business to conduct there. They were not persuaded.

But one day a teacher was raped—by an intruder. I was not there that day, but, on my next visit, the faculty told me—said it happened in the morning, before class, as the teacher was preparing to teach, when the halls were filled with noisy students, and the hall monitors, a few doors away, were having coffee, and didn't hear her scream.

After that, the female teachers and the female students paid more attention when they were alone, when they turned corners, when they went up and down the dark, narrow, graffiti-covered, steel and concrete stairways smelling of urine, to the department chair's office, to the restroom. They told me no word came from the front office all day, until it was time for school to be dismissed, and then someone announced on the intercom that a teacher had been raped that morning, "but no harm had been done."

The teachers who spoke to me were almost in tears. I couldn't bear to think of them feeling so alone and so vulnerable in their huge, dark, dirty, shameful excuse for a school, and discussed this with my college students. I asked for volunteers to go with me and do one symbolic, encouraging thing, ludicrous though it may appear, and may be: paint the faculty women's bathroom on the third floor bright turquoise, and put up a poster there.

One girl volunteered to go. We called the principal, informed him of our plans, drove three hours, visited classes, waited until school was out, told the custodians what we were doing, where we would be, and had that huge empty building to ourselves. We took all the time we needed, made that bathroom glow in the dark hallway, finished in time to leave when the custodians left, gave them our poster to put up the next day, when the paint was dry.

It was a purely symbolic gesture, all we could think of to do for all the women who were afraid, for all the women whose hearts and minds ached. We received phone calls, and thank-you notes, telling us that women from other floors had been making pilgrimages to the third-floor bathroom, because—because, at such times, when someone has crossed a line, and that line has not been properly acknowledged, and grieved, some kind of pilgrimage, no matter how ludicrous, is necessary.

MAPPING

In my first year as a visitor to the city school, I talked by telephone with the classroom teacher often. I learned that way that there were two riots with guns and knives at the school that year, and that everyone was afraid of what might happen next. It seemed to me as if everything were flying out of control there. I felt ridiculous, being a visitor in such a school, bringing college students with me to talk about college, with people who, in ninth grade, had already hidden in their classrooms while other students, from other classes, raced through the hallways shooting at each other, with people who, in ninth grade, had spent their language arts class screaming at their teacher, "Don't go near the door! You'll be shot!" How could anybody concentrate on studying spelling words and writing essays and term papers under conditions like that? What could I do with them in fifty minutes that would allow them to be calm, to be introspective, to take some time to regroup, to look beyond the class-room and the school? What, beyond the classroom and the school would they want to look at, would be encouraging to them, and not just add more anxiety to their already full-to-overflowing, anxious lives?

I told them that, at my school, we didn't have riots. I told them col-lege classes were quiet, and, in our building, with three floors of classes in session, you could hear the sounds your own shoes made as you walked down the hall. You could hear the sound of the chalk on the blackboard, the sounds of cars and trucks shifting gears on the road out of town, at the edge of the college campus. I told them no one ever shouted in our class, told them everyone had a chance to talk, every day, in the space of fifty or seventy-five minutes. I told them all schools were not noisy, told them there were schools where people could concentrate.

They stopped talking, decided to hear more. I said it was important to me to try to get to know them, because, really, people didn't exist in groups. They existed one at a time. Every person had a special personality. Even identical twins had special personalities. I had had several sets of twins in class, I said, and they did not think alike, or write alike, or have the same tastes. I said one way I could begin to know them would be to ask them to write. I said I would be thrilled if every single paper for me came out different from everybody else's, said it would be wonderful if no two were alike in any way. It would be all right if they decided not to put their names on the paper—just so what they wrote there was not at all what anybody else wrote.

I told them I often started my college classes in this way, asking how they felt about something they would probably not have written about if I had not asked them. I said, coming to this school, driving down so early in the morning, driving through coal country and farm country and industrial areas, driving first on tiny little back country roads, and eventually on the interstate or the turnpike, I had lots of time to think, and lots of things to think about, and often I found myself thinking how strange it was that human beings, wherever they live, whatever their age, have exactly the same emotions—the farmers, the truck drivers, the coal miners, the teachers, the students—the same. And one of the most common feelings in the world was the feeling of fear.

Everybody, I said, felt afraid sometimes. And, though there were times when you could never understand the people who created the circumstances of fear, you could always reflect on your own emotion of fear and try to understand and share that. Another feeling, I said, that I thought about a lot and that was hardly ever discussed anywhere was the feeling of being interested in something, even when no one else around you was interested in it. I said it was neat, how you could sometimes sit in a noisy room and be so interested in something that you would no longer hear any of the noise around you. And, finally, there was the feeling of happiness. Like these other feelings, happiness was something each of us felt in a different way. No one could tell us we shouldn't feel happy when we felt happy. It was not something we could do by "should." Happiness just happened—under certain conditions.

I wondered if they might share with me, in writing, at least one of these feelings—give me kind of an introduction to that feeling, from their point of view. I said they were welcome to write about small things or large things—I would be interested in whatever they decided to share with me. And I would not be thinking about things like spelling. What I wanted to know about was what they thought and felt. This is what they wrote.

*

My mom scare me because she makes me sick. She yells at me for every little thing I do for one thing I don't want to live with her no more because I'm scared I might hurt her. I want to live with my dad.

*

Dying is the thing that scares me the most. The thing that intrest me the most is Math and World History. In history I like learning about the past and how my ancesters lived. The thing that makes me happy is becoming a doctor.

*

The reason I like scary books is because when I read these books it makes me think that I am in the story and then I can imagine being there and acting as the person who's being chased or being killed and it's just interesting about how the people act and sometimes I think that the character is being stupid for doing things.

*

I get scared when I don't do the right thing and someone points it out.

*

I don't want to fail because I just not ready to go out on the street and try to make it on my own. If I don't do good in school I don't think you can make it in the real world.

*

I think that the life of musicians and actors is interesting because I like to know what they think about their fans and what kind of life they lead. Because I want to find out all I can about them, like how they feel when they're on stage performing, etc.

*

I'm happy to be a ballet dancer, and I'm also glad that I'm good at it. My teacher say that I may one day be able to help the other children in what I do. I like also helping others. People say that I'm pretty and nice. I like to think I am.

*

What makes me happy is getting good grades, I feel good and proud of myself. I feel as though I have accomplished something. That's why I always try my best in any subject, even if I don't like a certain subject.

*

Hi! I'm a naturally happy person and that's the way I look at life a stage of comedy with millions of striving comedians looking to find their way thru may fall off by the way side and then they would be the audience soaking up the new ideas so they get back on that stage and make something of the class act

*

I think school is intersting because of the classes I have. It's fun their the teacher's make the class speak up get to know each other. I like the activities at the school.

*

The things that are very interesting to me is wars of the past.

*

Money makes me happy because without money I would be bored. With money, I can buy all the thing I want and will be happy for days just as long as I'm not broke. I'm happy even if it's just 50 cents.

*

I think the most interesting thing I like is being able to work in a hospital and help people when they're sick. I think thats fun because you get to see and meet alot of people and being though I like to talk alot it'll really help me out in that aspect. Also I want to be independent and not lean on other people to support me. I'll be the 2nd person in my family to go to college so I be proud of myself.

*

Reading intrests me the most because its intriguing and fun. When I read a book I want to go on and on so that I want to know whats going to happen next. I love to read all kinds of things horror, romance, drama, and also informative things. I would like to become a Pediatrician and I know there is a lot of reading involved so Ill be prepared because its fun.

*

Writing make me happy Writing helps to express how I feel if I have a problem and there's no one to talk too, I just write it down on paper to release some tension.

*

Ging makes me happy. I really like sing. Also my parents deeing scares me because I will not have anyone to help me. Egypt interests me I like it and have people lived. I like the religion that also interest me.

*

Basketball is my interest. I really want to make it in basketball I'll be trying out for my school team this year.

*

Something that scares me is electricity because I'm afraid of getting shocked because I could imagine its painful. Something that makes me happy is traveling to different places and seeing new things. Something that interesting is study diseases and medicine and there effect.

*

I feel happy when my mom sees my passing grades. She's happy I'm happy and if I had a failing grade my mom would give me a lecture. I'm not about to listen to some long lecture. Because she did it to me when I was in eighth grade and had to go to Summer School she gave me a lecture.

*

What I thought was very interesting was how the Egyptians built there pyramids and how they carved the faces out of stone. What is so interesting is that they didn't have any sandblasters or anything strong enough to carve such things.

*

The thing that interests me most is the brain. Or in other words how they act and think about others and themselves. I like analyzing people and there emotions and ideas and hopefully that will one day help me become a successful psychologist for young teenagers who are full of emotions and ideas.

*

I think life is interesting. It's because I never know what's going to happen next. Life also helps to keep me on my toes. Most of the time I like what happens next. Sometimes though I don't like it.

THE RIGHT SIDE OF THE BRAIN

My left-brained colleagues, I suppose, did not often appreciate my view that school, by ignoring the right half of everyone's brain, made learning tedious and dull and passive. But most *students* loved it, thought it was amusing and weird and off the wall and silly and fun and adventurous to realize that this undeveloped part of them was *there*. They all showed me how they doodled in their margins, how they drew trees and race cars and snowboards and themselves and members of the opposite sex and the beach and parties with their friends—always— with their *left* brains, which were formulaic, which were structured, which were logical, which preferred a systematic, even judgmental, ap- proach to everything, and which were, therefore, not much suited to art and music and play and humor, and yet were pleased to have a try at such playing anyway.

When college students drew, they hummed to themselves and tapped their toes or bounced their heads in time to music that was inaudible to the rest of us. If they were tired and preoccupied before, they forgot that. They were engaged. If they were angry and irritated about a test or a teacher or a paper or a boyfriend or girlfriend, or anything else, they put that aside now, sighed with relief, prepared to enjoy themselves. They were not proving anything. They were not being tested on anything. They didn't have to memorize anything. They could relax and just be in the present and follow where their awareness and feeling and imagination led them. If I decided to teach them drawing for the rest of the semester, they would happily attempt whatever I asked them to do. It felt surprising, playful, luxurious to them—just to explore, just to play, in this way. They didn't believe they had talent in this area, and yet it didn't matter. They expected it to be an adventure. They could visualize themselves as artists having an adventure. It was a pleasure to put the pressures of their lives aside for a while, float down this new river on this brand new mental raft that nobody ever paid any serious attention to before.

The new high school students were no different. I asked them, as I had asked my college students every semester, to draw a tree, a house, and a flower—draw them any way they wished, draw them from any angle, draw them any size, make the flower huge, if they wished, make the house small, the tree ordinary or peculiar, put the house in the tree, or the tree in the house, or the flower in the tree. I predicted that *all* of them would use their *left brains* to do this drawing.

They had no idea how I would be able to tell. They had no idea what I would be looking for. So, like the college students, they assumed I was measuring their talent, and, like them, they thought they *had* no artistic talent, so they laughed. They laughed at themselves and at each other. They didn't expect anyone in the room to be good at this. It was liberating. It was like going bowling for the first time and being absolutely certain that the whole class would roll gutter balls.

I walked around the room, watched the drawings emerge. No matter if this roof was shaped like a triangle and this roof was a parallelogram. No matter that this was concrete block, and this was wood, and this was stone, and this one had a bay window, and this one was a row house, and this one had an apartment over the garage. They were all *left-brained*. I was ninety-nine point nine nine percent certain that this would happen.

I enjoyed their drawings—empathized with them, remarked on this detail or that, celebrated *everybody's* drawing, enjoyed their lollipop trees, their tulips that looked like little sawblades with curves under them, their daisies that resembled each other but did not resemble any daisies in this world. I watched as they carefully and happily drew identical curtains in each window, drew knotholes in their trees, added birds' nests, added birds in the air, added smoke curling out of the chimney, added a sidewalk leading to the door. They could add details like these all day and it would still be a left-brain drawing.

Now that they were finished, they wanted to know how I could *tell*. I went to the board. I drew a formulaic house, a lollipop tree, put in my own details, all with exaggerated over-simplification. They *saw* that it was all stylized, it was all formula. Nothing we had drawn looked like things really look. Our drawings were only *reminders* of the "real world," short cuts, the same short cuts we took in elementary school—because that was the last time we thought about ourselves as artists, and because no teacher ever told us about our right brains or showed us how to use them.

I passed around Betty Edwards's *Drawing On the Right Side of the Brain*, marked pages of "before" and "after" drawings, proof that this approach to drawing *worked*, that people drew beautifully in just a few months—once they learned how to access and use their right brains. In the time remaining, I did a few of Edwards's exercises with them, showed them how to draw a "face vase," how to do a pure contour drawing. I brought in flowers. We drew them. I asked a student to volunteer. I drew the student on the blackboard without looking at the blackboard, showed them what it felt like to pay attention to the way the lines go, showed what I saw when I paid attention. I asked them to divide into teams of two, draw each other in that same way, without cheating, without looking at the paper.

Half of the class sat perfectly still as the other half drew. They expected near-perfection, because they *saw* near perfection. They saw faces, saw them clearly, in detail, from less than two feet away. When they finished, and "looked," they laughed, felt a little foolish. They saw that, of course, they had had no idea where their pencil had been, and had drawn noses over elbows, by chins, outside the face. No matter. They felt what it was like to *look*, to see edges where their classmate's hair seemed to touch the wall, where the collar touched the neck, where the upper lip touched the lower lip. They realized that they could *draw* those edges. It was just that they didn't yet know how to keep track of where they *were*, where their lines were, in relationship to the rest of the drawing. They could learn that, though. After all, hadn't they just drawn in a totally fresh way? Hadn't they just demonstrated that they could do this, and could see that they had done it? The lines were *there*, on the page, exactly as they had seen them. They were just, often, in the wrong *place*. That was incredible, really. Incredible.

This was not, of course, a drawing class. This exercise was just to demonstrate that, all day, they studied and learned, or were supposed to be studying and learning, but never in their lives had they studied and learned with this part of themselves—until now. Now they knew what it meant to "have potential."

Wouldn't it be fun, if they had a chance to develop that other part, for even an hour every day or so? Wouldn't it be delightful, to relax like that, to experiment, to see where such experiments might lead? Who knows? After a semester or so of practice, they might decide to change their major to art.

WHITE PEOPLE ALL LISTEN TO CLASSICAL MUSIC

I was sitting in on an English class. The teacher was reading Shakespeare aloud because there were not enough books to go around. Some students followed along in the books there were. They liked it when he read. He read with imagination, understanding, pleasure. It was not a duty. He asked questions about the characters, about the plot, about the theme, to see if the students were with him. They were.

Suddenly, out of nowhere, I heard him telling the class that white people always listened to classical music. I was the only white person in the room. All eyes but his looked in my direction. I raised my eyebrows, said nothing. No one else said anything either. He went on with his reading until the bell rang. The students filed out. I stayed behind.

"Gee," I said. "My parents don't know a thing about classical music. They listen to Bing Crosby, and Lawrence Welk reruns. I learned about classical music in fourth grade, when my teacher persuaded my father to let me play the violin. Don't you think this means that we don't know each other well enough? I don't think either one of us is going to fit a stereotype."

He grinned, pulled out his wallet, took out his business card with his home phone number on it, and handed it to me. I gave him my phone number.

The next time I visited, the students told me how boring school was. Same old, same old, they said. "Hm-m-m," I answered. "I bet you

weren't bored last time I was here when the teacher said all white people listened to classical music. I bet you wondered whether I did or not."
   They laughed. They were not bored now either. They wondered what
I was going to say next. I had thirty-some high school students' attention. I told them my classical music story, and asked them how many
white people they knew, besides me and a few other teachers. None.
One boy said there was a white homosexual in his neighborhood, so he
assumed that most white people were gay. Someone else said she'd
seen a lot of white people on television, and they were all rich, and
wore nice clothes, and drove nice cars. I asked them how many white
teenagers they knew. None. Not one. Not to the slightest degree. Not
even the name of a white teenager.
   I told them I had an idea, which I had been thinking about since the
last class. "It's easy to stereotype other groups when we don't know individuals in that group," I said. "Not all stereotypes are negative, but
all of them are *inaccurate*."
   "The next step," I said, "seems obvious to me. We need to bring individuals from different groups together, get to know each other. Would you
like to do that? I could match you up with white high school students, put
you with people who seem to approach things the same way you do, so
you'll feel as if you have something in common. What do you think?
   "You could be pen pals with each other next year, come up to the college for a day and meet your pen pals. We could have a writing workshop at the college for students in both groups, help all of you to have
an understanding of what college writing will be like, what you will
need to learn by the time you are ready for college. Then we could apply for a grant to bring you up for a week in the summer.
   "You could choose a couple people to be your class representatives.
The other school could do the same. I could take those people up for a
weekend to help plan these things. They could stay overnight with representatives from the other school. Your representatives could relay
back to you what they do, how they feel about what they learn about
the other students, about the town. How about it?"
   They all thought it was a great idea. They were not bored anymore.
They were actually going to meet white teenagers, write back and forth
to them, get to know them. Next year was going to be an adventure, was
going to be full of surprises. They were going to be part of the surprise.
   Can you *believe* that?!

"GOING OUT NOT KNOWING"

I had a grant from the social equity office of the state system of higher education to ferry a class of white students from one school and a class of African American students from another to the college for the week of July 18–25th. There was enough money in the grant to pay for every student. I had asked the two groups of students to spend the school year writing to each other, had brought representatives of each class together for a weekend to brainstorm about what should happen during that summer week. We had already spent a day at the college together in a writing workshop for all the students, with college students as mentors. We were as ready as we knew how to be in the time we had had to get ready in.

The grant application said that my goal had been to help students to have a positive self-image and to maintain their hope that they could go to college and enter the careers they wished to enter. It said that, to this end, I had visited their English classes regularly for two years, and had brought them to the college campus twice to work with college students and faculty. It said that, this year, to help break down racial stereotypes that might interfere with their concentration on school, I had paired the city students with students from a local high school. Now they would come together for intensive work in composition, art, and science. They would work together in both formal and informal settings to do college-level work in composition and, with college students and faculty, design and carry out projects in both science and art. The high point of the week would be a camping trip to a nearby lake, where, in beautiful natural surroundings, they would complete their projects. This summer enrichment experience would give them a wonderful opportunity to know their pen pals and to have close contact with college students who would serve as their big brothers and big sisters. As a result, racial stereotypes would be broken down, confidence in their ability to write and think would be increased, and self-esteem would be enhanced.

I wrote to the parents of all sixty students, told them about this grant, sent them registration forms, explained everything that needed to be explained. I arranged for two mothers to accompany the city students on the bus and to return to the city with the bus driver or to spend the week with us, as they preferred. I wrote to the college students who had signed up for the summer composition section, explaining what I would be asking of them, ordered science project supplies: electrodes, electrocardiograph paper, electrode gel, calipers; ordered art supplies: fabric, dyes, waxes, t-shirts, drawing tablets, pencils; ordered writing supplies: journals, pens, typing paper; arranged for camping supplies: tent rentals and camping sites for ninety students.

I had arranged for two science professors to show students how to measure their percentage of body fat and their heart rate on an exercise bike and a treadmill. I had arranged for a counselor to lead a discussion of emotional stresses associated with college, arranged for an art professor and his family to teach us all to tie-dye at least one t-shirt each. Other art professors helped me to select and order the supplies. I had organized a "rap session" so project students could discuss anything they wished with interested college faculty and college students for an hour every morning. I had arranged for all the necessary transportation, had made a map of the campus, had purchased folders for each student, and ordered copies of all necessary information for them.

The spring semester was over. So far, I had received only two of the sixty registration forms back from the city students' families and seven from local students' families. I began to call all the remaining families, asking for an update on the status of their registration forms. Some told me that their child was participating in basketball, soccer, football, or cheerleading camp that week. A few had decided to participate in other college enrichment programs closer to home. The rest of the families expressed doubts about the program. The parents of city students told me that they were afraid that it would not be safe for their child to stay in the home of a white family. They were afraid their child would be robbed, or attacked, or even raped. The parents of the local students said exactly the same thing. Several also told me that they thought what I was doing was wonderful, but that they themselves were not ready to participate in something like this, were not ready to have a member of another ethnic group in their home.

Some city parents, thinking there might be safety in numbers, asked if their child might come with a classmate and stay overnight in groups of two. I told them that would be fine. I said I'd make sure that they had the address and telephone of the host family and that the host family had theirs. Some said their child had a summer job and was afraid of losing it for a week-long absence. I offered to write a letter on college stationery, explaining the program to the employer. Some said they were afraid that the college workload would be too much for their child, and the child would be bored or discouraged. I went over each activity, explaining what would happen, explaining how lively and fresh every activity would be, how carefully paced the schedule would be, how it would include plenty of time for touring the town and swimming and sports and picnics and getting to know host families.

On June 17th, there were still only nine students registered for the July program. I wrote to each family, went over all this information again. I called the nine who had registered, to be sure they were coming. I spent the rest of the month and part of July trying to find host families. I had only *one* local host family from our school district, one pen pal's family. At this point, all I needed was one more.

I called family after family, spoke with parent after parent, asked them if they might reconsider. I had the most amazing conversations about racism—about their fears of "the other." Those fears were deep, and sharp, and vivid, and powerful. These were the *parents* of high school students. They must all have been at least forty years old. None of them could imagine taking this step. None of them could think of *anything* that would persuade them to take it.

I told all this to the drive-in teller at my bank, in another school district, told it with amazement, with sadness, with disappointment. She said she had three teenage sons, all of them active participants in sports. All of them, she was certain, would be comfortable with an African American student. All of them would *love* to have the second student as their guest. Her husband would welcome him too. The second student was a basketball player. It sounded like a match. She promised to call me in the evening. She did. The whole family was excited about this unexpected adventure. They welcomed it.

I continued calling others, as back-up. I talked to local ministers, asked if members of their congregations might help us. No one came forward. And no other registration forms from the city families arrived. On July 11, I cancelled the bus. I would drive the three hours each way and pick up the two students myself.

My college students were looking forward to the week. They would all love to tie-dye a t-shirt. There would be plenty of t-shirts. If I made one, and if the art professor and his family made one, there would be at least seventy-five t-shirts left over. All twenty-five college students signed up for the tie-dying. All of them encouraged me, told me it would be fine, promised to be there for all the activities, promised to make sure the high school students felt welcome and had a good time.

There were only a few days before the program was to start. There was nothing else for me to do. I went to bed every night at ten, slept eight hours, walked five miles every day in the early morning, went to class, hoped for the best, hoped—that is—that the two city students would be at the school parking lot when I arrived there on Sunday to pick them up.

JUST SAY YES

On Sunday, July 18, I left my house at five A.M. in order to arrive at the city high school by eight o'clock, the time when the bus to the college would have left. Our opening session was scheduled for eleven o'clock.

When the students learned that they were the only two going, they said they didn't want to go; they wanted to go back home with their families. All of us—two mothers, two fathers, two students, and I— stood in the empty parking lot and talked. We talked about the fear of going—of being so alone, and so vulnerable, and so trusting. We talked about the advantages of going anyway, about the advantages of staying home, about the disadvantages of going or staying. All the parents felt strongly that the two should go, understood thoroughly how hard it was going to be to drive away, to leave their kids with me, to let them face their fear. They all understood why the other families could not do the same. It was up to the students. They thought about it. They felt how it felt. They decided to go. It was not a happy decision. It was a sad, scary, lonely, painful decision. They walked to my car, loaded the trunk with their luggage, kept their Walkmen, sat in the back seat together, listened to their Walkmen the entire three hours.

The college students, the other high school students, and the two host families were there to greet us. They cheered. They were excited, happy, just a little nervous. We went inside for punch and cookies, sat in a circle, eating chocolate chip cookies provided by the campus dining hall, talking about our fears and our hopes. Everyone there spoke. Everyone there was honest, trusting, real. Everyone there felt how helpful that was. We talked for over an hour, then the host families went off with their guests, the other students went home, and I walked my five miles by myself. I had nothing to do until the next morning.

On Monday, the two city students skipped the rap session and came late to the science class. They had spent that time in the campus bookstore, marveling at the abundance of everything there but textbooks—the t-shirts, the sweatshirts, the running gear, the souvenirs, the posters, the magazines, the art supplies, the trade books, the candy, the cases of soda, the shelves of cheese and crackers and yogurt and soup and ice cream. No class could compare with all that. We talked to them, assured them that we saw their side, but reminded them that we had put hundreds of hours into preparing for this week, and its success depended on their presence. There would be time for the bookstore. We promised.

After that, they were there for every session, and everyone else was too. The college students were right. The week went perfectly. The guests liked their host families, felt comfortable with them. The host families took them everywhere they could think of—to miniature golf, to go-cart racing, to the nearest amusement park. They played basketball, swam in the town pool. Everyone participated in all the classes, in the pizza party, in the picnic at the lake. They loved the tie-dye class. One student stayed there twice as long as he was required to, and made two t-shirts, one for each of his sisters.

At the end of the week, everyone was sad to leave. They had had a great time. They had participated in everything, talked about everything they could think of, could have stayed another week.

I drove the city students back home. This time, they talked the whole way, laughing, smiling, could hardly wait to show their families the tie-dyed shirts they were both wearing. We drove into the school parking lot. It was not the same parking lot it had been a week before. It was a place, now, of celebration, of triumph. Everyone hugged everyone. Someone asked where they got the t-shirts. They said they *made* them. Made them! They took another look. Made them! They had never made anything like that in their lives. "They're *beautiful!*" one mother said, the amazement and pride clear in her voice. "They're beautiful! I can't get over it!"

THANK YOU

It was graduation day—at last. We were downtown, in the basement of the Civic Center, where all the seniors were helping each other into their graduation gowns, adjusting their tassels, and saying their last good-byes to their favorite teachers. The teachers looked forward to this day, not because it was the end of the school year, not because they had shepherded another group of boisterous teenagers safely through the school system, but because it was so wonderful to feel so appreciated, to be hugged and thanked by so many happy kids, by the same happy kids who had exhausted them and kept them awake at night and tried their patience for the last four years. I had been here four years. I was part of this too.

This was the real celebration. The dutiful ceremony that followed, upstairs, couldn't compare with this, with being surrounded by sixty smiling, laughing, eager eighteen-year-olds, all of them wanting to hug you at the same time, all of them finding their own way to say a thank you that was so contagious, that felt so real, so happy, so high on their list of important moments. Never, in all my years as a student, and all my years as a college professor, had I seen or been part of anything like this. In my experience, students at graduation were the center of attention, felt relieved, felt encouraged, felt proud of themselves, felt lucky, felt free, felt eager to get on with their lives. They hugged their families, hugged their boyfriends and girlfriends, hugged their friends—but whole classes of them did not hug their teachers, and they rarely thought of thanking them.

This was the last group of Health Academy students who had gone through a review and selection process to be admitted. The rules had been changed. After this, the Academy would have to accept anyone who wished to be admitted—whether they had an interest in health careers or not, whether they had any special talent or motivation in this area or not, whether they were at all academic or not. When students were evicted from one school and sought admission in another, they would have to be taken in—even if they had been found guilty of violent or criminal behavior, even if their chances of acting out and disrupting the class were a hundred percent. In addition, those who managed the academy would be given more responsiblities, not fewer, and smaller budgets, not larger. They would have to administer the program—and also cover the classes of their colleagues who were absent—cover them, that is, *themselves*, and teach their own classes as well.

The teachers were worried, angry, bitter, resentful. What would happen to the integrity of the program they had worked so long and hard to maintain? What would happen to the special assemblies, the special class trips, the special links with local hospitals? What would happen to their graduation rate? To the quality of their teaching? How could you teach if your room was filled with students who didn't want to be there, who didn't care about learning, who were preoccupied with other things, who just took up space and distracted those who were trying to learn? How could you teach if the students' quick tempers, their hopelessness, their desperation, seemed out of control, were out of control? How could you concentrate on what needed to be taught and learned when you were afraid for *your* life? When your students were afraid for theirs? When nobody had the energy to think about what they were supposed to be *there* for?

They did not look forward to the next school year. For this reason, more than any other, I decided to take on one more group of ninth graders. I wanted to see if I could distinguish them, academically, from the first group. I wanted to see if they felt as hopeless about themselves as their teachers expected them to feel. I wanted to see if I could encourage both the teachers and the students, if I could encourage the school as a whole, help it to see itself differently, help it to feel how it felt to see a bright side, as well as the other, more familiar, more frustrating, discouraging, sad, frightening, hopelessly lost in the mires of bureaucracy and political punishments and favoritisms side. And I wanted my college students to spend more time in the city, with the city students. I didn't want them always to be the hosts, the leaders, the teachers. I wanted them to understand that the more active learning is, the more important it is — and the more important it is, the less likely it is that it can be measured. I wanted them to realize that high GPAs were meaningless, were absurd, unless the mental and emotional and spiritual work you did to earn them mattered to you for its own sake.

It was my last chance to teach here in this way. I had decided, finally, to retire at the end of the school year, to give myself a rest, to give myself a chance to think, and write, about what I myself had learned in devoting some thirty years of my life to teaching mostly students who had not considered themselves students, at the beginning, who had not come to college primarily to learn — in any holistic, real, important, self-changing, and life-changing way.

I spent an entire day with the new high school students, had a headache after only second period. In all their classes, they sat in rows, filled out worksheets, took objective tests, were expected to do everything everyone else did, at the same time, in the same way. As the day went on, they became more and more unruly, more and more tense, more and more frustrated. Education! What is that, to so many students who didn't see any value in memorizing vocabulary words, in studying spelling words for a weekly test, when they had so much more painful and meaningful and urgent things to think about? These papers, these tests, these books—they meant nothing to them. They felt trapped, angry, bored. They felt invisible, isolated, and alone. How could they possibly endure this for four more years?

How could they believe that their teachers understood them, and cared about them, when most of their day, almost every day, consisted of rote learning, busy work, and lecture, lecture, lecture?

I watched, saw clearly which teachers cared, and which didn't. I watched these students "take a test," saw them get up out of their seats, in full view of the teacher, walk across the room, look at a friend's paper, go back to their seat, write the answer—saw them whisper answers back and forth, as the teacher remained at her desk, absorbed in some other business.

This year, they had a computer class. For security reasons, they had to leave their regular classroom when they did computer work, go to a different room, in the middle of the class period, unlock the door, start class all over again, get out their assignments, boot up their computers, copy a paragraph correctly. The students had perhaps ten minutes left of the period, by the time they were ready to copy the paragraph. They spent more time booting up than they did typing. It was a boring, unimaginative paragraph, a "the book is on the table in the classroom" paragraph, not one worth such fuss. A few succeeded in copying it. Most of them did not. One paragraph. They put away their work, planned to finish it another day, left the class, having accomplished nothing, went on to their science class, the last class of the day.

These thirty people, all supposedly headed for careers in the health field, sat slouched in their science class, as the teacher droned on and on and on, making no attempt whatsoever to engage them, seeming not even to notice, or care, that they were not engaged.

Watching them, I saw how four years looked to them, how they stretched out like a desert ahead of them, a dry, empty, hopeless, unnurturing place. I wished I could think of a way to build an oasis.

REPRISE

*

I am so tired. I'm glad I made it to 15 years old. I am glad I am perfectly healthy. It was a blessing. Hard to get through school. All the violence coming to a end.

*

I feel tried. I glad I'm good Group. I live my uncle. It was very good. Have sex. Make me feel good.

*

I'm so tired. I'm happy I was born. I'm happy school is all most out. That my brother was born.

*

I am in a alright mood, not happy not sad. I was happy when I got of suspention.

*

I'm not feeling well, at the age of 14 I want'a do well. I want to have money with-out to jail. My memeries make me feel good, the nineth grade is hard to pass but I know I could, I notes makes me feel good.

*

I feel good that I was born in this world and I lived to be 15. When I stayed in New York I met a famous rapper. I was happy. When I got drunk and high that was hard for me to deal with.

*

I talk on the phone all night long the phone is my talent.

*

My talents are dancing, acting, modeling, helping others, and talking on the phone.

*

I'm not feeling so well. My birthday is next Friday and I'm happy to have lived another year. I met my boyfriend. This is relly nice cause I'm getting a touch of life! My uncle has ben dead for 6 years. Triumphs, hardships, and Labor.

*

Woo haa: Busta Rhymes. Energetic. When I was 11 I could get my hair done at a solon. When I was 13 my curfew was later at 11:30. Delightful.

*

I think my talent is talking because I like to talk alot and I can talk anyone I see.

*

I feel sleepy. I found $200. I met my best friend. They were realy realy cool. I think about me and my future.

*

Its been long time coming but I know, change gone come.

*

"Jesus Don't Want Me For a Sunbeam" just pops into my mind when I'm in deep thought, sometimes.

*

Mad me. Alone. F— up. Bloom times. Mad killer. Kill-me. I am the bad boy. Here is my handwriting.

*

I'm in a lolly dolly happy mood, happy that I was able to swim up and down the blue water, so good that I can swim now. Sing "Lift Every Voice and Sing" makes the water waves flow.

*

I'm feeling very glamarous. In a fact I'm 14 but in the mind I have I wisdom of my age backwards. People would always seem to get along with me. These things are great to me. When I am in school people would always judge me without knowing me and that's [stress].

*

My mood is sleepy. I am glade I was born. I am glade to have nice things. They're very wonderful. I think about my grandfather's death. I think about nothing.

*

I'm so mad because I didn't get money from my dad. I'm happy to be alive. I think about being free and being above all the depression and everything else that people go through.

*

I feel so happy and sleepy today. I'm sixteen and I was glad I was born. I am glad when I had my first birthday party. They were good feelings. I think about when I almost got in trouble in school.

*

I am happy and energetic. I was glad when I was brought into this world. I was glad when I got older because I was able to do more exiciting and interesting things. The memorys of my life had a good ending and feeling. The tough part of my life has something to do with growing up.

*

I feel very hungry.

*

I am full of joy. I was happy when I started school, I get to do what I want. I feel okay, not bad at all. I think about when my aunt die.

*

I can sing. I can draw. I am helpful.

*

Chillin. Really don't know. Uh-h-h. I think about death.

*

My mood today is good I want 2 all beef patty, special sauce, lettuce, cheese, on a sesame bun. The first time I'm happy when I am talking to my boyfriend. The second time is when I am spending time with my mom. I think about freedom, life, growing up.

*

My mood today is ok. I felt happy when I go out with my girl friends. I feel happy when I'm with my family. Life was hard when I don't have no money. "Lift Every Voice and Sing" is a good song it like a earth song.

*

My mood today is good I feel happy today. When I was 14 and I met my boyfriend and we have been going together almost 1 year. Another time when I been happy is when my sister had my niece & nephew. A time when life was hard was when my grandma die and when my boyfriend went to job core & left me.

*

I think the world today is crazy, all the people fighting and killing each other. I would rather be with my grandmom up in heaven.

SYMBOLS

I'm thinking of these kids now—ninth graders, fifteen. I'm thinking about how they've told me they feel: tired, tired, tired, tired, sleepy, not well, not so well, mad, alone, hungry, would rather die. Glad they "made it to fifteen." So many like that. And yet, other kinds of gladness too: glad to be born, glad to have birthdays, glad to have good memories, glad to have talents, glad to feel glamorous, to have energy, to be a talker, to swim, to imagine change will come, to be older and do more, to start school, to be with friends, to have a boyfriend, to be free, to sing, draw, be helpful.

Not an easy life, not a carefree life, not a life to take for granted—but the only life they know.

How easy it is to get caught up in the details of the day, whether they are happy or sad, complicated or simple, and not look too far beyond them.

Perhaps because I drive from one school to another, and back again, perhaps because I listen to college students, and then high school students, and then college students again, over and over and over, I can't help staring into the chasm that separates these two places, can't help trying to understand how it came to be that way.

It's money, partly, of course. All the other schools I've visited have plenty of books, plenty of paper, pencils, paper towels, bathroom tissue. No other school I visit is covered with graffiti. No other school lawn is filled with weeds and trash. No other parking lot is littered with broken glass. You don't line up to be searched when you enter any other school. Teenagers who don't belong there don't lounge outside the doors, anywhere else.

I never saw the principal of this school walk up and down the halls of this huge, depressing, ugly place. I never saw him stand at the dirty, wire-reinforced, two-story windows that looked out on the expanse of weeds that all the rooms on that side of the building looked out on, never saw him shed any tears over the despair and emptiness inside.

But, if you look at it, if you really look at it, your heart hurts. It hurts for the kids who don't know that most other schools, in spite of their problems and their deficiencies and their lack of humanity, are not nearly this bad. Your heart hurts for the kids who never get a chance to make music in this school because, though there is "a music wing," there is no music class, and no choir, and no band, and no orchestra. Your heart hurts for the kids who never get a chance to make art, because there is one art teacher for three thousand students, and there are a few loaves and fishes to trade for supplies, but no miracles. Your heart hurts for the kids who are years behind their peers in other schools in their reading and writing, and who could profit from special reading classes, and volunteer adult tutors, and peer tutors, and college-student tutors, that the school can't afford, or can't find, or doesn't look for.

It hurts for the kids who have never seen a modern library with useful periodicals, a library where most of the books are not forty years old. It hurts for the kids who are expected to enter the computer age without any state-of-the-art computers anywhere in the school, for the kids who want to study science, but who have no science labs, and no equipment, for the kids who want to go into journalism, but who don't even have a school newspaper, or a yearbook, for kids who might want to study radio and television, and who, every day, pass by a room marked "television studio," which has never, ever, contained anything even remotely related to a television studio, which is used, instead, as a storage room.

It hurts for the teachers, many of whom have devoted their entire adult lives to these students, and who know that everything they have given is not enough to make the kind of difference that needs to be made, who know that there are never enough textbooks, or enough teachers, or enough resources, who know that they are rarely consulted by the administration on campus, or the administration downtown, or the administration at the state level, about what should and should not be done to help these kids learn, to help them catch up, to help them thrive.

It hurts for the department heads, who must find substitutes when any teacher is absent, and who know that the only substitutes they will probably find will be themselves. It hurts for those who lose staff, and who lose funding, and who lose autonomy, and who lose choice, when they know that staff, and funding, and autonomy, and choice are the only sane alternatives to the authoritarian and unjust system we have now.

It hurts for the principal too, because it knows that it would not be easy for such a person to see these things, and to feel so totally responsible for all of them, and so totally helpless, and so totally alone.

I was not responsible for any of these things. It is just that I saw them, and felt how it felt to see them. It is just that I listened to what the students said, and listened to what the teachers said, and listened to what the principals said, and I stood at these windows every day I was there, pressing my forehead against them, trying to think of some small way to alter this bleak and shameful view.

So that's how I came up with the idea of a garden—a real garden, with real perennials, and real flowering shrubs, and real trees, and real benches that real people could sit on, and feel real sun, and real breezes, but a symbolic garden as well—a garden that spoke of space and nurturing, that spoke of perspective, of alternatives to constant noise and confusion and aimlessness and emptiness and futility, a garden that spoke of replenishing resources, of anticipation and celebration of seasons, of simple, natural beauty and peace.

Sometimes no one knows how exhausted we become when we try to enlarge our own resources to meet the needs we see everywhere around us. I knew so many others had overspent. I myself had overspent. In my dreams now I stood at the entrance to the subway downtown, with my students—all the high school kids, all the college kids—lined up on each side. I dreamed that all of them were looking at me, with their hands out, their palms raised, waiting, waiting, waiting, waiting. In the dream, I reached into my pocket, closed my fingers around my last dollar.

I felt immensely sad in the dream. How is it that we do so much, that we do all we can, and that the need does not diminish? How is it that we long to go on, that we see it as our responsibility to go on, with nothing to go on with?

Upon waking, I saw what needed to be done. I am small. We are all small, by any measure. There was only one thing to do: ask others for a dollar. Ask only for that. One dollar. How many dollars could we collect? How many flowers could we buy? How many students, how many colleagues, could I persuade to come with me? "Literature and Society," my two literature classes were called this semester. Many, in my department, taught this class for General Education students, students who wanted an English elective that didn't quite sound like a traditional English course. "Quite" was not the word for it, in this case. I knew that.

I took the position that *we* were society, that *we* brought about social change or we didn't, that we got rid of prejudices or we didn't, that we measured our lives against literature, and literature against our lives, and sometimes we could not help but conclude that it was our lives that needed to change. I ordered copies of *Poetry Like Bread: Poets of the Political Imagination* and asked students to subscribe to *Real Change*, Seattle's newspaper for the homeless, certain that none of my students would have been exposed to these writings before, certain that reading them would remind them that the world outside textbooks was larger, and more challenging, and more precarious than any of us could know or imagine, and certain that we would feel connected to this world.

I told my students of a public garden that I had visited many times, that was large enough, and natural enough, and quiet enough, and beautiful enough to balance these other worlds, and invited them to go there with me, to feel how such balance felt, and to see where it led.

And I told them about the view from the window, and asked if they would be willing to share the public garden with the students there, become pen pals with them, visit back and forth with them, and join them in creating a garden of their own.

Only a few dropped the course. Sixty-three remained. There were fifty-eight ninth graders. I asked them. On a scale of one to ten, I said, where ten is wonderful and one is ridiculous, what number would you give this project? Almost all of them gave it a ten. The lowest score it received was an eight. We met. We talked together. Pen pals corresponded.

A bus from the college and a bus from the high school arrived at the public gardens. Two by two and four by four, students went out into all that green and growing space to see what a vision might be made of, learned something about their tastes in flowers, learned where many of the flowers originated, were surprised that some came from Africa. They had not expected that, had assumed that Africa was all poverty, and war, and starvation.

Altogether, we collected more than four hundred contributions of a dollar. I matched that, bought flowering shrubs and perennials, loaded them onto a bus in April. We arrived with shovels, buckets, drop cloths. We filled the space outside the windows—over a hundred of us—college students, high school students, teachers, the principal, the bus driver, the policeman, the grounds crew—all digging in the dirt, all loading weeds onto drop cloths and into wheelbarrows, creating a twenty-foot circle in the center, semicircles around the edges. Except for a short lunch break, we worked all day, transforming that space.

"I never thought it would be so *large*," the principal said. Some of the students worried that plants in the garden might be destroyed. Some were. We found them, pulled out of the ground, lying next to the holes they had made. One of our trees was broken in two. We replaced the broken ones—once, twice, three times. The next fall, we planted three hundred tulips. The following spring, when they bloomed, a teacher washed the windows.

During the next year, after I had retired, teachers and students from another department in the university accompanied me to the high school. The grounds crew built a fence around the garden. A biology teacher and her students adapted the garden to their needs. Sometimes, the high school students and teachers, and former college students, gathered in the garden to pull weeds, or to have their pictures taken there, or just to talk.

On these occasions, some of the younger students always asked: "Why do the weeds grow faster than the flowers?"

I wish I knew, and I wish I could have told them. A symbol is only a symbol, and sometimes its energy is soon spent. But some of us who spend our lives teaching know that, even though we spend everything we have to spend, we will never keep pace with the weeds, and the best we can say, and know, is that at least we were on the side of the flowers, and we understand something about the attention and care they require.

References

Baldwin, James (1965). Sonny's Blues. In *Going To Meet the Man*. New York: The Dial Press.

Branden, Nathaniel (1981). *The Psychology of Self-Esteem*. Toronto: Bantam Books.

Cameron, Julia (1992). *The Artist's Way*. New York: G. P. Putnam's Sons.

Chapman, Abraham, ed. (1968). *Black Voices*. New York: New American Library.

Cronyn, George W., ed. (1962). *American Indian Poetry*. New York: Ballantine Books.

Cummings, E. E. (1968). *Complete Poems: 1913-1962* (First American Edition). New York: Harcourt Brace Jovanovich, Inc.

Edwards, Betty (1989). *Drawing On the Right Side of the Brain* (A Jeremy P. Tarcher/Putnam Book). New York: G. P. Putnam's Sons.

Espada, Martin, ed. (1994). *Poetry Like Bread*. Willimantic, CT: Curbstone Press.

Fromm, Erich (1956). *The Art of Loving* (Perennial Library Edition). New York: Harper & Row, Publishers.

Frost, Robert (1949). *The Complete Poems of Robert Frost*. New York: Henry Holt and Company.

Ginott, Dr. Haim G. (1975). *Teacher & Child*. New York: Avon Books.

Hemingway, Ernest (1961). *The Snows of Kilimanjaro and Other Stories*. New York: Charles Scribner's Sons.

Henri, Robert (1960). *The Art Spirit*. Philadelphia: J. B. Lippincott Company. Compiled by Margery Ryerson.

Holt, John (1967). *How Children Learn* (First Dell Printing). New York: Dell Publishing Co., Inc.

Holt, John (1969). *The Under-Achieving School* (First Laurel Edition). New York: Dell Publishing Co., Inc.

Howe, Reuel L. (1963). *The Miracle of Dialogue.* New York: The Seabury Press.

Jersild, Arthur T. (1952). *In Search of Self.* New York: Teachers College Press.

Jersild, Arthur T. (1955). *When Teachers Face Themselves.* New York: Teachers College Press.

Joseph, Stephen M. (1969). *The Me Nobody Knows* (First Discus Printing). New York: Avon Books.

Kesey, Ken (1962). *One Flew Over the Cuckoo's Nest* (A Signet Book). New York: New American Library.

Koch, Kenneth (1970). *Wishes, Lies, and Dreams* (First HarperPerennial Edition). New York: HarperCollins Publishers, Inc.

Lewis, Richard (1966). *Miracles: Poems by Children of the English-Speaking World.* New York: Simon & Schuster, Inc.

Lewis, Richard (1969). *Journeys: Prose by Children of the English-Speaking World.* New York: Simon & Schuster, Inc.

Masters, Edgar Lee (1962). *Spoon River Anthology* (Collier Books Edition). London: Collier-Macmillan Ltd.

Miller, Ruth, ed. (1971). *Blackamerican Literature: 1760–Present.* Beverly Hills, CA: Glencoe Press.

Moustakas, Clark E. (1961). *Loneliness* (A Spectrum Book). Prentice-Hall, Inc.

Moustakas, Clark E. (1966). *The Child's Discovery of Himself.* New York: Ballantine Books.

Moustakas, Clark E. (1975). *Psychotherapy With Children* (Perennial Library). New York: Harper & Row Publishers.

Neill, A. S. (1960). *Summerhill.* New York: Pocket Books.

Neruda, Pablo (1974). *Extravagaria* (First American Edition). Tr. Alastair Reid. New York: Farrar, Straus and Giroux.

Prine, John. "Hello in There." Miami, Florida: Warner Brothers Publications.

Randall, Colvin (1995). *Longwood Gardens.* Kennett Square, PA: Longwood Gardens, Inc.

Rogers, Carl R. (1961). *On Becoming A Person* (Sentry Edition). Boston: Houghton Mifflin Company.

Rogers, Carl R. (1969). *Freedom To Learn.* Columbus, Ohio: Charles E. Merrill Publishing Company.

Rubinstein, S. Leonard (1966). "Composition: A Collision With Literature." *College English*, 27 (January, 1966), 273-277.

Steichen, Edward (1955). *The Family of Man.* New York: The Museum of Modern Art.

Thompson, Lawrance (1970). *Robert Frost: The Years of Triumph.* New York: Holt, Rinehart and Winston.

About the Author

Nancy Gill is a Pacific Northwest artist and writer who works with at-risk students in their homes in her home state of Washington. She graduated *summa cum laude* from Grays Harbor College (1962) and Washington State University (1964, 1965) with degrees in English, earned her Ph.D. in English from The Pennsylvania State University (1979), and taught composition, creative writing, and literature courses at the university level for over thirty years.